HICK 'N' DILLEY CIRCUS

HICK 'N' DILLEY CIRCUS

Graeme Hick
and
Graham Dilley

with Patrick Murphy

MACMILLAN
LONDON

First published 1990 by
MACMILLAN LONDON LIMITED
4 Little Essex Street London WC2R 3LF
and Basingstoke

Associated companies in Auckland, Delhi, Dublin, Gaborone,
Hamburg, Harare, Hong Kong, Johannesburg, Kuala Lumpur,
Lagos, Manzini, Melbourne, Mexico City, Nairobi, New York,
Singapore and Tokyo

ISBN 0-333-53317-8

A CIP catalogue record for this book is available
from the British Library.

Phototypeset by Rowland Phototypesetting Limited
Bury St Edmunds, Suffolk

Printed in Great Britain by
Billings Book plan Limited, Worcester

CONTENTS

ACKNOWLEDGEMENTS

Hick 'n' Dilley circus. All right, it may be a rather laboured pun, but the English first-class cricket season *can* be a bit of a circus. All that travelling, the compulsion to entertain, the regular frenetic bursts of activity, the showy performances that conceal a good deal of hard practice – and the presence of a few clowns in the spotlight. When we agreed to keep this diary of the 1989 season as it applied to Worcestershire and (hopefully) in Dilley's case to England, we hoped that it would not sound the death-knell for Worcestershire's prospects. For some reason, cricket diary books seem to jinx the particular player's season and that of his county. Think of Bob Willis in 1978, Brian Brain in 1980, Graeme Fowler in 1985 and Jon Agnew in 1988. Not one trophy for the county concerned in any of those summers.

Luckily, the 1989 season proved a dramatic, controversial and ultimately successful one for Worcestershire. The melodramatic pressure of South African rands on current England players added an extra dimension in the case of Dilley. As a result, whenever I met up with my colleagues, we wondered just how we could summarise the hectic events of the summer. I have tried to put their opinions at the time within the context of the season as it progressed, from freezing, rainy Lord's in mid-April to freezing, rainy Pontypridd in mid-September. I have not given Hick and Dilley the chance to be wise after the event, choosing to allow myself that option instead. Seems only fair: I had to ask all the questions and boost the profits of a certain audiocassette manufacturer!

My sincere thanks to both Graeme Hick and Graham Dilley for their professionalism and friendship during the summer – without them etc. etc. etc. Also to all those Worcestershire players who said at various stages, 'Don't forget to ask them about . . .' To the Worcestershire secretary Mike Vockins for wielding the censor's blue pen with the finesse of a fencer. Mike's indefatigable assistant Pauline Boyce was equally patient with my ceaseless requests for scorecards and photographs.

Any literary praise accruing from this book will be exclusively claimed by me while all complaints ought to be addressed to G. A. Hick and G. R. Dilley, c/o Worcs CCC. They get enough glory during the season. I now consider myself the world's leading authority on Worcestershire's 1989 season. I wonder if Magnus Magnusson would accept it as my specialist subject.

PATRICK MURPHY
WORCESTER, NOVEMBER 1989

INTRODUCTION

Graeme Hick and Graham Dilley approached the 1989 English season with varying degrees of optimism. For Dilley, the elder by seven years, there was the awareness that his career at Test level was drawing to a close. For a fast bowler with suspect knees, a thirtieth birthday is a time for reassessment and a realistic acceptance that the skill of surgeons cannot keep the machine ticking over smoothly for too many seasons. Graeme Hick faced challenges of a different nature. Not yet twenty-three, he was now saddled with the tag of being the best young batsman in the world – yet it would be another two years before he could attempt to go up another gear and prove himself in the Test arena. Born in Zimbabwe, he had decided to embark on a seven-year qualification period for England. A couple more years remained, two years during which Hick would be trying to scale new heights of prolific efficiency.

The conventional wisdom is that bowlers win championships, but Graeme Hick had reversed that trend the previous year. Without his runs, Worcestershire would not have had the time or the confidence to bowl sides out twice. That Hick played so many marvellous innings on home pitches that unduly favoured seam bowling only underlined his immense value. The last championship game of the season at New Road was the best example of his worth. Worcestershire needed all four batting bonus points against Glamorgan to be sure of winning the title in the face of a spirited challenge from Kent; it was safe to assume that Glamorgan would be beaten, but full points would give Worcestershire a one-point victory in the championship. Hick made his usual hundred, then took fresh guard and, when he was finally out for 197, the full quota of points was assured. That was the last in a series of virtuoso performances in 1988 from Hick. There had been the 212 against Lancashire on an Old Trafford pitch that turned sharply, the 405 not out against Somerset at Taunton that proved to be the highest score in England since 1895, and the 172 against the West Indies that took him past a thousand first-class runs in May, the first time this had been achieved since 1973. Within a few weeks of that historic Taunton innings, Worcestershire supporters were sporting T-shirts with the '405 not out' motif, and Hick's bat manufacturer, Duncan Fearnley, had shown characteristic flair by stamping the same legendary inscription on his new range of bats.

For Graeme Hick, the 1989 season was programmed as another step on the road towards batting greatness. He knew better than anyone that all the eulogies he had earned since making his Worcestershire début in 1985 would be worthless unless he made the progression towards acknowledged Test class. Senior professionals on the English county circuit would add just that one rider to their glowing assessments of Hick: judgement had to be reserved until he had faced, and mastered, the West Indies fast bowlers in the heat of international combat. Only a handful of batsmen – Bradman, Woodfull, Ponsford, Merchant – had surpassed the young man's record of a hundred every five innings, but they had also met the challenge of Test cricket. Until then, Graeme Hick would continue enjoying life in English cricket's most handsome ground, savouring his privacy in his modern detached house just a mile from New Road and clocking up runs in metronomic fashion. The winter of 1988/9 had been another time of personal and professional satisfaction: Christmas at his parents' home and then the serious business of making runs. Another high-scoring season with Northern Districts in New Zealand had shown that the acquisitive hunger had not been assuaged. By the start of the new season he appeared ready to delight both statisticians and connoisseurs again as another English season began.

Graham Dilley has rarely been able to approach a long season in the same optimistic vein as Hick. The unnatural strains placed on a fast bowler's physique, coupled with an attitude to the pain barrier that has been far from stoical, meant that Dilley has grown used to long spells on the physiotherapist's couch. In his later years at Kent – before he moved to Worcestershire in 1987 – Dilley had appeared less than fully committed to the cause. Too often he had taken the easy option and decided he was not fit enough to play. That was a reflection as much on his unhappiness at Kent as on his true physical condition. He had never forgiven the Kent committee for sacking Chris Tavaré from the captaincy in 1984, and his relationship with Tavaré's successor, Chris Cowdrey, had been uneasy over the next two years. When Dilley agreed to join Worcestershire he was the genuine article as a fast bowler, possessing pace and swing. All he needed was the heart, the resistance to niggling injuries to back up the undoubted class that invariably made him the best bet to dismiss top-order batsmen. Although still troubled by injuries in 1987 and 1988, Dilley had made a significant contribution to Worcestershire's championship win. In the last month of the 1988 season, it was clear that he preferred playing for Worcestershire rather than England, and his readiness to play despite chronic pain from his right knee impressed insiders at Worcester. Those who knew him maintained he had never been happier with his cricket since his move.

That serenity did not apply to his time with England, however. The unhappy tours of Pakistan and New Zealand in 1987/8 had disillusioned Dilley. He resented a fine for an audible obscenity uttered on the field during a Test in New Zealand and asked to go home. He was disturbed by the attitude of the English authorities to the Shakoor Rana affair. When Mike Gatting was sacked from the captaincy in the summer of 1988 over alleged nocturnal activities with a barmaid during a Test match, Dilley was aghast. He had played many successful games under Gatting and by the end of the 1988 season he was disenchanted with the way English cricket was being run. He was not dispirited when the winter tour to India was called off for political reasons. A winter at home would do him good, perhaps restore his appetite for the international fray and give him time to have surgery on that troublesome right knee. An operation in September was pronounced a success and it appeared that England's best strike bowler would be ready for the Australians. He had bowled beautifully against them in Australia in 1986/7 and his late swing was sure to trouble batsmen such as Steve Waugh, David Boon and Dean Jones who sometimes played across the line. All the pre-season predictions about the forthcoming Ashes series featured the likely impact of a fit Dilley on Australia's top order. His continuing well-being was very important to England.

Yet Dilley was not only troubled by his right knee. He knew that a difficult career decision would soon have to be made. South Africa beckoned and this time he would be trading in his Test future for a hefty sum of money if he agreed to go there again. January's special meeting in London of the International Cricket Conference had established that any players who went to South Africa faced bans of up to seven years. Dilley was certain to be a prime candidate for any unofficial English tour. He had gone on record to admit that the biggest mistake of his career had been to turn down the South African Breweries Tour under Graham Gooch in 1982, because that would have brought him financial security. Dilley also sympathised with the efforts made towards multi-racial cricket in South Africa. He had played out there for Natal and had enjoyed the experience. Moreover, he was now clearly disillusioned with the Test scene and a ban would not affect his contract with Worcestershire, where he was enjoying his cricket so much. In short, Dilley was ripe for plucking if a tour were to be arranged. The early part of the 1989 season would be full of such rumours. The press would be at its most inquisitive and the money involved would be cranked up by the rumour machine to huge sums.

Both Hick and Dilley are professional enough to submerge their individual aspirations within the team ethic at New Road. They knew that they were integral parts of the outstanding side of 1988 and they were hungry for more. There had been justifiable criticisms of the New Road pitches during 1988 and there seemed little prospect of a vast improvement in 1989, but apart from that it is hard to deny that to win the Britannic Assurance championship, the Refuge Assurance title, and to be runners-up in both the NatWest Cup and the Refuge Assurance Cup constituted a remarkable season. These are heady days at New Road, where the press box bulges with luminaries, and it is advisable to get there early for a satisfactory vantage point. The club's car-park attendants battle to shoe-horn every vehicle into the ground, the trade at the bars is brisk, and the commercial officers rake in the sponsors.

INTRODUCTION

Worcestershire is now one of the better-run clubs in the county championship and the players enjoy the extra exposure which comes from being successful. With Ian Botham returning for the 1989 season after a year's absence with a serious back injury, there seemed no doubt that the 'Car Park Full' notices would be a feature of the summer.

PATRICK MURPHY

PRE-SEASON THOUGHTS

Before the co-diarists began recording their season in mid-April, they assessed each other's qualities. One of the interviews was conducted in an immaculately kept lounge over coffee to the strains of Belinda Carlisle on compact disc, the other over some splendid Australian Chardonnay and a full ashtray in a pub garden. The master batsman and the country's best fast bowler may inhabit different social worlds, but Hick and Dilley have genuine respect and affection for each other.

DILLEY ON HICK:

Those who have met him briefly all say the same thing – seems a nice lad, a bit shy, a credit to his parents. Well, he's all of those things, but he's a lot tougher than people realise. In the dressing room he won't take any crap – you've got to be sure of your facts before you can have a go at him successfully. He'll stand up for himself, even though he's so young. He knows what he wants from cricket and where he's going, and that's a major plus to know that at such an early age in a career. At Worcester we're all encouraged to speak our minds and at team meetings Graeme contributes a lot. There are a few loonies like me and Ian Botham, a few brainy characters (four university graduates, don't you know) and relatively inexperienced ones like Graeme who are fine players and therefore confident about expressing their views. Graeme takes the same amount of leg-pulling as the rest of us and he gives it back in a quiet, dry fashion. He plays cards in the dressing room (a silly game called Anaconda Poker, where the highest hand and the lowest hand win), and he'll enjoy a few pints on an away trip with his room-mate for the past four years, Damian D'Oliveira.

Yet he never goes over the top: you only have to look at him to see how hard he trains.

Graeme's not moody if he fails. I've never seen him out of form, unlike lesser mortals, so it'll be interesting to see how he handles a bout of bad luck or bad form – assuming it ever strikes him. People ask me if he can make it at Test level when he qualifies. I haven't the slightest doubt that he'll do it. He has everything that makes a Test batsman – ability, technique and temperament. I bowled at him in New Zealand in 1988 when he was playing for Northern Districts and it was an interesting experience. He made 140-odd on a flat wicket and none of us seemed to be able to bowl a dot ball at him. If you bowled wideish at him he'd just run it away and if you bowled on the stumps he'd hammer you. I'd walk back thinking, 'That wasn't a bad ball, yet he's hit me for four,' and that is one of his strengths. Around eighty-five per cent of the bad balls go for four and the good ones often disappear as well. He plays very straight and, because he rarely misses out on the bad ball, he just wears you down. Graeme exerts psychological pressure on the bowlers, like Viv Richards or Javed Miandad. It all depends how you can handle that: when I first started, Viv Richards used to intimidate me, but as I got older I realised that such a player will inevitably have more good days than bad. Bowlers lining up against Graeme Hick must also come to terms with that.

Some people reckon Graeme's vulnerable to a ball that comes back from outside the off-stump. I've lost the ability to do that over the years so I wouldn't have much chance of getting him out that way. When I've been bowling well in the nets I've got him with one that leaves the bat, but I have to be at my very best and get it in exactly the right spot. It'll be harder for Graeme to score masses of runs in Test cricket but even if he has a bad trot he'll get through it with some ease because he has such a lot to fall back on. If he had joined another Test country he'd now be on his way to the quickest thousand runs in Test history and he'd be the youngest to do it. England is very lucky to have got him.

Some ill-informed knockers suggested that he lacked the right temperament because he failed at Lord's in last year's NatWest Final – but he was bowled by a very good performer in Angus

Fraser on a helpful wicket. So what? He proved his temperament by getting that 150-odd against the West Indies to get past a thousand runs in May on a bad wicket. Some people talk a load of codswallop. Too many uneducated folk write and talk about cricket – they thumb through the dictionary, come to 'T' and write down 'temperament' instead of staying at 'talent'.

Not only am I certain that Graeme Hick will be a great Test batsman – I'm also sure that he'll be able to handle all the ballyhoo. He'll be coming up to twenty-five then and, although everyone will be wanting a piece of him, he's so mature and sensible that he won't get carried away with all the fuss.

⊗ HICK ON DILLEY:

When Graham Dilley joined Worcestershire in 1987 I wasn't quite sure if it was a good signing or not. I thought our bowling was strong enough and I remembered a game when he was playing for Kent and he seemed to get easily discouraged after I had hit him for a couple of fours in one over. I wondered if he was too easily discouraged, but I realise now that he was unhappy at Kent and his bowling just wasn't together. Since he came to Worcester, he's done really well for us. I think he's a great guy. He likes to be in the background, enjoying all the banter in the dressing room, puffing away at his fag, coming in with a wry comment at just the right moment. Graham's not one to seek centre stage. He knows a lot more about the game than he lets on. He'll tell me if I'm not using my feet properly in the nets, he won't throw the coaching book at you but just offer a few quiet words.

When I stand at slip I really admire his rhythm. The run-up and delivery seem so effortless, it all seems to explode in the last couple of yards. When he's going well he lines up the target, starts the ball on middle stump and swings it late away from the batsman – and that's the killer delivery for a good player. Last season when we played Yorkshire in the Benson and Hedges Cup, Graham showed his class against two good openers, Martyn Moxon and Ashley Metcalfe. They could hardly lay a bat on him, the ball was beating the outside of the bat by almost a foot. Dilley 1 for 10 in nine overs and I was glad to be watching it from slip, rather than trying to cope with him. He and Neil Foster are the best English opening bowlers – Fozzie does it more off the seam while Graham is quicker and swings it devastatingly when everything is right. In pre-season nets Graham always turns us over, bowling us off-stump while we aim towards mid-wicket. Mind you, we're convinced that in the nets he bowls at us from nineteen yards, dragging through the crease. He seems to swing it a lot later when he's not bothering to bowl legitimately! We shout 'no-ball!' as he pings the off-stump, but he just grins and points to the debris behind.

Some say that Graham gets too easily discouraged, that he sulks on the field. I've never seen that, he simply gets disappointed and annoyed with himself. It must be hard on a fast bowler to get nicked through the slips to the boundary off a good ball, especially after running all that way and using up so much energy. Graham's no different from anyone else in that he needs a fair amount of encouragement. There's no one near to him as he plods back to his mark, so we all shout encouraging words to him from behind the wicket. We need him to come back strongly in the last hour of the day after working hard for spells of eight overs or so earlier on. No wonder he's a big sleeper in the dressing room. He's on a par with Kapil Dev, the great Indian all-rounder who was at Worcester when I first started. He'd lie down on the floor, put a couple of towels behind his head and go to sleep with his pads on, saying 'Wake me up when it's my turn to bat.' He never bothered about assessing the bowlers, he just woke up and batted. Graham's a bit like that – although I reckon Kapil just shades him!

On the eve of an English season that was to last five months, Graeme Hick was still coming to terms with the burden of being labelled England's great hope for the future. Undoubtedly during the two years that remained before he finally qualified for England he would dominate bowlers while playing down grandiose forecasts that England's international fortunes would be transformed as soon as he stepped on to the field for them. After another prolific season in New Zealand with Northern Districts he joined Worcestershire on a short tour to Hong Kong, Singapore and Australia, designed to tone up the county champions for the new domestic season. Yet the day before the new English

season started with the champion county playing the MCC at Lord's,
Hick was troubled by more than a lack of match practice due to
Brisbane's tropical storms.

 HICK:

I've been offered a lot of money to return to Australia later in the
year to play Sheffield Shield cricket with Queensland. They came
in for me after New South Wales offered, then withdrew, a package
that would've worked out very handsomely for six months once
you throw in air fares, rented accommodation and a car. Although
that hasn't worked out, Queensland appear to want me. They're
not offering as much, but I'm not worried about that. I just don't
have the right feeling about the deal. Professionally the prospect
is attractive because the cricket out there will be harder than in
New Zealand, where I've spent the last two winters. Yet things
aren't being handled properly from the Australian end. When I
was getting ready for Worcestershire's tour, I had a call from
Graham Thomas, managing director of Carphone in Australia,
who have a tie-up with both Worcestershire and Queensland. I
didn't commit myself to the deal at the time, even though I also
talked to the chairman of the Queensland Cricket Association,
Alan Pettigrew. I told both gentlemen that it all sounded fine in
principle but that I wouldn't commit myself until I had talked it
through with them in Brisbane. Then Graham Thomas tells the
press that I've signed for Queensland. It even got on Teletext back
in England. That was rubbish.

When I finally got out to Australia I talked to the Queensland
officials and initially there was a stumbling block. I asked them
for a couple of air fares for next winter, for myself and my
girlfriend Jackie. I understand it's a standard request from any
overseas player and it is usually granted, but they only offered me
one economy ticket. Eventually they agreed to my request but by
then I wasn't sure that Queensland really wanted me. I talked to
Allan Border, the state captain, about it and he merely said that
the time out there would be good for my cricket and that I'd enjoy
it. He never gave out total encouragement – maybe if he'd said
something like 'Come and join us, we want you' then I might

have felt I had his total backing. Meanwhile Ian Botham offered to negotiate for me with the employers who had sacked him a year earlier. Beefy [Botham] thinks I'm being undersold on the Queensland deal, but I think I'll keep him away from all that!

While I mulled over the Queensland situation, New South Wales came in with a better offer. At least a committee man has made me the offer. I know Bob Radford from a trip he made to Zimbabwe, and when I laid out my terms he said right away, 'You've got it.' He was talking about a very generous salary for six months' work. Unfortunately the story has leaked out and the New South Wales committee has rejected it. Perhaps the players are unhappy about the deal, perhaps the other officials feel they should've been consulted by Bob Radford, but I imagine Bob wanted to move swiftly before Queensland closed on it. But do Queensland really want me? I know it'll be hard for me out there, because I lack the international stature of someone like Ian Botham. They still haven't won the Sheffield Shield in over sixty years of trying and I assume they see me as the guy who could help them do that. A lot of overseas players have gone there and not really shone in Sheffield Shield cricket and I know that out there, they don't rate you until you've performed well against Australians. All the runs I've made elsewhere matter nothing to them.

The money isn't all that relevant – after all I would go to Queensland rather than New South Wales if all of it works out and they're offering me less. I feel as if I'm sitting in a shop window with people walking around me, taking a good look. In recent years I've always felt that getting things right out on the park is the vital aim and financial considerations will then take care of themselves. I handle my own cricketing contracts and I don't worry unduly about the noughts on the bottom line. It was more significant that I felt isolated during the negotiations in Australia – I didn't really know the people I was dealing with.

To make matters worse, I didn't get a run on this Aussie trip with Worcestershire. In five knocks I've had two noughts and a one. I threw myself under pressure out there because I wanted to do well now that it's been announced that Queensland are after me. I've wanted big scores too badly. If I had got some runs to show them my capabilities it would make it easier for me later in the year if I came back. Otherwise I'll be under greater pressure, especially when people read about the details of my contract. If it goes ahead, all I want to be is a respected member of the team, someone who will pull his weight over all the responsibilities – but I have this nagging sense of misgiving about the whole thing.

From a cricketing point of view, this trip didn't work out for Worcestershire. The weather was awful and we've missed ten days of hard, concentrated pre-season training back in England. We need good nets in the morning, followed by some long sessions at fielding practice, getting ourselves dirty by diving around. We should have gone out to Australia a week earlier, played some competitive cricket and returned to get used to English conditions again. Now we will be lagging behind other counties in their preparations for the new season: I hope that doesn't show because we owe it to our members, our supporters and to ourselves to prove that we haven't only been having a good time on tour. There are a few important games early in the season and we don't want to be eliminated early from the Benson and Hedges Cup or start slowly in defence of the championship. Yet a few days before we begin the English season, we had to resort to racketball or squash to burn off excess energy because it was raining in Brisbane and the indoor nets were just not safe.

As for my England qualification, there had been a rumour earlier in the winter that my waiting period would be cut. In fact an English journalist rang me up at three o'clock in the morning in New Zealand to check my reaction to the meeting at Lord's. I told him that my qualification period would probably stay the same and I was proved right. He told me that one county wanted me to play for England now, but that I'd have to wait another two years before I could be deemed an Englishman for my county. In other words they were against Worcestershire signing another overseas player as soon as I was deemed to be English. Ridiculous – looks like they're worried about Worcestershire getting even stronger. That would also mean I could proudly wear an England cap and sweater but forget all about that for two years while I was playing county cricket as an overseas player!

I have no complaints about having to wait until 1991 before I qualify. A long time ago, I decided that an England cap was my goal, provided I was good enough. I might have qualified for New Zealand sooner, but playing at Lord's for England is the pinnacle. As a kid I used to read about the battle for the Ashes and great players getting hundreds at Lord's and I was fired up by that. All top cricket seems to hinge on the Ashes. It must be great to walk out to battle against the Aussies. I've even allowed myself the fantasy of wondering who I would be alongside when and if I play for England. I'd love to walk out at Lord's with Ian Botham at my side and others I respect greatly like David Gower, Mike Gatting, Allan Lamb and Graham Gooch. I just hope their hunger for runs is still there in 1991. They've played so many Tests in recent years, I suppose the appetite must get dulled.

I'm so hungry to do well at the highest level that I don't want to lose the chance. I know that I won't be fulfilled as a person until I've been tested in the Test atmosphere. In the last few years, I've watched a lot of Test cricket on television and I sit wondering what it must be like to play in it. I don't expect to clock up big scores like I do in county cricket but it'll help if I get off to a reasonable start because that might help change the minds of those who never wanted me to play for England in the first place.

Ironically, I might have been eligible for England last year if my parents had taken an opportunity that was available in the early seventies. They could've gone down to Pretoria and collected British passports, but they felt they'd hold on to their Rhodesian passports – they saw no need to change, they had no idea that their young son would be useful with the bat! So that might have helped me play for England after four years' qualification, rather than seven, because I would have held a British passport. But I'm happy with the way it's gone. Coming over to England at the age of seventeen has given me time to get used to everything. It's better for me to learn about the connected things – like dealing with the press – rather than have to learn as I go along if I get into the England side. I do read the papers – the tabloids for my own entertainment and the serious ones to cut out articles about my career to send home to my parents, who keep scrapbooks about me.

I suppose my prevailing mood at the start of another English season is one of confusion. I'm mixed up about the Queensland situation and I also feel I'm not properly prepared, due to a lack of hard training in English conditions. I'm there to be shot at because of last year's success and the same applies to the team. It's always harder to defend a championship than win it for the first time, so I hope we can pick up the momentum quickly after our disappointing trip to Australia. When we start tomorrow at Lord's we mustn't think about coasting along, even though it's just the MCC match. The hard work starts here.

Graham Dilley also had food for thought as the team settled into their London hotel beside Lord's. Due to political considerations, England's tour to India had been cancelled so Dilley, along with the bulk of his England team-mates, had kicked his heels at home. In Dilley's case, that involved time at home in rural Worcestershire and occasional convivial evenings with close friends in local hostelries after a day's clay-pigeon shooting. After the operation on his right knee in September it would have been touch-and-go whether Dilley would have been fit for the Indian trip, and the pre-season tour with Worcestershire had done little to convince him that he was physically ready for a new domestic season. He also knew that a proposed unofficial England tour to South Africa was now likely and that he would be a target.

⊘ DILLEY:

I'll have to take seriously any offer from South Africa, even though I dearly want to get fit for England this summer. I don't really see any moral problems here. It's been made quite clear at January's ICC [International Cricket Conference] meeting what's in store for anyone who plays out there, so the black countries have had their pound of flesh. It seems odd to me that our tour to India was called off because of Graham Gooch's connections with South Africa, yet he hasn't been there for years. But businessmen can trade with South Africa every day and no one says a word about them. Unlike the placard-wavers at college, I've actually been out there and seen what cricket can do for blacks. If Ali Bacher is involved in any possible England tour, I'll be even more tempted, because he is a great cricket administrator who has done fantastic work for players of all colours. Talking to players in the England team and around the circuit, it's clear there's vast sympathy for people like him and he'll have no trouble getting a decent English side out there. I'm certain he'll make sure the money's right to compensate us for ending our Test careers. We'll all be watching this one with interest – should be some good gossip around the dressing rooms!

But that's only a possibility and, for the moment, my loyalties are all with England. My knee is a worry. The right one first troubled me in Australia in 1986, when I missed the Melbourne Test. A year later it bothered me again in New Zealand. I delayed an operation on it till September last year because it was important to me to help Worcestershire clinch the title. The last few weeks of last season were a trial but it was worth it. So the surgeon opened me up, and cleaned out the offending areas, but it was still not right when we went to Australia. Basically the knee gives way sometimes when I run in, and I know that I shan't get through this season without surgery.

It's an important season on a personal level – the Ashes and all that – but I don't want to let down a county that's been good to me and given me a great deal of happiness in the last two years. I've enjoyed the break this winter but I know I'm not as keen on cricket as I ought to be. I'm not enthusiastic about all the off-field complications associated with the game, and in that sense I have a lot of sympathy with Ian Botham. I'd like to be able to do my job without being so visible, but I suppose that's asking a lot of someone who's six feet four, with long blond hair, and who bowls fast. It doesn't bother me if my name is not in the papers – there are times when I would just like to be a normal guy in public who's not recognised. Now I only go to places where I feel safe socially and rely on a few friends to help me unwind. I regret that, but there's nothing I can do about it.

Many say that my heart doesn't match my ability, that I should sweat and strain more and look as if I'm going through agonies for my side. That may have been true just a few years ago – I admit that towards the end of my time with Kent I wasn't giving of my best – but since I came to Worcester, I've tried bloody hard to get on the field whenever possible and do my best. I've come to the conclusion that people will write whatever they want about me and I'm never going to shake off the generalisation. I don't let it bother me now as I plod back to my mark, deliberately walking slowly so that I can plan my next delivery and get some oxygen into my lungs. If the critics applied the same standards to other sports, Chris Waddle would never have played soccer for England, or Nigel Clough would never have got into Nottingham Forest's team. When I first started with Kent, people used to say, 'Look more enthusiastic,' and I'd answer, 'How the hell can I look what I'm not?' I ended up telling them, 'Go and get someone else if you're not happy with me.' I really do now try my hardest when I'm bowling and, if they want someone to rush around who can't bowl, that's their problem.

Many don't want to be fast bowlers because it's bloody hard work. Whatever you do in professional sport has to be hard, otherwise everyone would be doing it. The fast bowler is rarely free of niggles like a blistered heel, sore feet, a tricky groin – yet you're expected to be hostile towards the end of the day when everyone else is tired. Plus the occasional heartache of being smashed around. The fast bowler just has to choose the best way of tackling all that. Superficialities like how keen you look just shouldn't come into it. If everything worked out right every day and I swung the ball at speed and put it in the right spot, then I'd take a stack of wickets, but the game isn't like that.

I remember John Snow telling me that a fast bowler has to throttle back when the wicket is flat but you have to go for it when the conditions favour you and you're expected to pick up 5 for 30. The worry can then be greater, as you may fail to pick up wickets in favourable circumstances. It's a question of being level-headed, taking advantage of the various purple patches and realising that you can easily take only one wicket in the next two games after you've bagged twelve in one match. I've always tried to be unaffected when successful, but I've fallen down when doing badly. That's due to a lack of confidence and I expect to be dogged by that in the coming season. I continue to take the good days a hell of a lot easier than the bad ones. The Australian tour in 1986/7 helped me: I finally broke the barrier of taking five wickets in a Test innings and I graduated from a four-runs-an-over man to a successful strike bowler, because I could swing the ball away from the bat consistently. It was all about confidence: we knew that we would beat them and that I'd get good batsmen out because I was bowling so well.

Now we have a new England captain in David Gower and a new chairman of selectors. I know little about Ted Dexter, although from what I can glean he seems to be one of those people who are born lucky. Is it the wheel of fortune in operation when a soccer manager takes over a struggling side and they soar up the table, or is it inspirational leadership? The same will apply to Dexter if he turns our fortunes around. He will have nobody different to pick from than Peter May, but perhaps he is the kind of talented guy who makes things happen. Certainly the media are enjoying the new era of *glasnost* with a new chairman and captain – I wonder how long they'll stay sweet with each other. My main success for England has come under Mike Gatting's captaincy and from a selfish point of view I had a very good chance of playing under him this summer if I'd been fit. I also knew he was a fan of mine.

I'm not too sure about what David Gower will want: Jon Agnew must now have a better chance of being selected because his county captain is also the England leader. If Aggers bowls brilliantly for Leicestershire he must play for England because David will be standing at slip to observe it all. Having said that, I have the utmost respect for David Gower. He is popular, down-to-earth, not egotistical at all. He handles himself and his fame very well and works hard at human relationships with his players. He has the kind of humour I enjoy and I like the fact that he is always there for a chat if you need him. I also agree with his philosophy that a Test player should be able to work out his technical problems by himself and that you shouldn't fuss around a guy good enough to play for his country unless he specifically asks for help.

I've lined up my rivals for the England team and there are a few. Neil Foster is talented, uses the seam very well and doesn't lack confidence. I remember his first tour – to Pakistan and New Zealand in 1984 – and in team meetings he'd say things I couldn't believe were coming from a guy on his first tour. Even then he thought he should be in the Test side. A few years earlier I'd just keep my mouth shut, but Fozzie was playing in a successful Essex side where you were encouraged to look after yourself, expected to get the new ball and the choice of ends. That attitude hasn't exactly harmed him. Angus Fraser is a very fine bowler and will press us all this summer. I think my county colleague Phil Newport will do brilliantly because he swings the ball and because the Aussies aren't very good against the ball that moves around. Alan Igglesden of Kent is going to be a top-rank performer if he can get through this season without too many injury problems. A definite tip for the West Indies tour. Greg Thomas has the speed and the attraction of a new county, although he has one or two technical problems that he needs to sort out. Gladstone Small is always there or thereabouts, although he often seems to be the one who drops out at the last moment, often through no fault of his own. A fair crop of contenders and I want to make my place secure, if I can just sort out my knee problem.

Our pre-season trip to Australia was a waste of time in terms of preparing us for the new campaign. I said as much last year when it was first discussed: you're in alien conditions, too close to the English season, and we'd be far better off staying at home, getting used to slow wickets. But it was a fun trip, the best I've ever been on in terms of getting to know each other even better, and I hope that our excellent team spirit will get us through the inevitable bad days when loss of form and injuries drag us down.

All the talk in Australia was about Ian Botham and his fitness after his back operation. Would he be the same player again? Did he want that? Well, he looks very fit and clearly he's worked very hard, with all those long walks to build up stamina and lots of racketball in April to sharpen up reflexes. Don't forget that his back should be right now because he's had a fusion and it should be stronger than many other backs on the county circuit. Beefy may look slim and keen but I don't think he looks right for cricket. He hasn't practised enough, he's behind in his nets work. I'd like to have seen him work more in the nets, rather than building up his stamina. After all, he's always been very strong. I said to him, 'Why don't you have a net?' and his answer was: 'I had one in the winter and it did me no good.' Typical.

He's always been very difficult to argue with, but a few of us will take him on. Sometimes he'll just throw up his arms and walk away, and that's the nearest you'll get to him admitting he was wrong. He starts off with a conviction that he's right and blusters those who won't stand up to him. Phil Neale, our captain, handles him well, trusts his judgement and yet goes his own way. Tim Curtis took him on after our first match in 1987 at a pub near Worcester. Beefy offered a drinking contest. I dreaded someone suffering but, although Tim lost, it was good to see one of Beefy's new colleagues stand up to him and not be in awe of the guy. As a result, Beefy has missed us during his year off, because he knows that a few of us in the dressing room will argue the toss with him. I think he'll eventually be fit enough to play for England again but perhaps not this summer. To me he is far behind in his cricket training, despite his great natural ability.

It will be interesting to see how we handle the burden of being defending county champions this year. I never used to believe in all this North/South divide till I came to Worcester, but now that we're slap bang in the middle of the country, I can feel that many people don't want the trophies to head south. Even though Worcestershire possessed a few glamour names, I sense that ours was a popular win because we were still deemed an unfashionable county. We are also close to being a very well-run club. Everyone has a moan at times but I tell our lot that it could be a bloody sight worse. My experience at Kent has taught me to be grateful to the administration at Worcester, particularly the secretary Mike Vockins. When I was at Kent, we lacked self-belief because in the last decade we were too worried about what was going on off the field. That's why the Kent lads were ecstatic last year to finish second to us in the championship: they didn't expect anything like that, yet they finished just one point behind us. They had become conditioned to mediocrity. At Worcester we expect to win, we back our bowlers against any other attack. And we also have Graeme Hick.

EARLY SKIRMISHES

Worcestershire returned from their Australian venture to the earliest start to an English first-class season since 1903. Just forty-eight hours after stepping off the plane, the champion county lined up at Lord's against an MCC side containing several players with an eye on the Australian Test series ahead. Graeme Hick, still worried by the offer from Queensland, chose the match to remind everyone of his qualities with a scintillating 173 not out in Worcestershire's total of 474 for 3 declared against the MCC's 281 for 4. He also had to contend with a scare story about his period of qualification for England, after playing for Zimbabwe against a touring Australian side.

HICK:

I had a call from a journalist while in Australia and he suggested that I might have broken my qualifying period by playing for Zimbabwe in 1986. Obviously I was worried, but Mike Vockins, the Worcestershire secretary, had already assured me I was in the clear. He told me I could still go back and play in Zimbabwe because it wouldn't be first-class cricket. I could play in their domestic cricket but not in the World Cup or the ICC competition. Mike Vockins told me to keep checking with him over any future games that might affect my England qualification and that's what I've done. But it was a relief when the word came from Lord's that I was in the clear.

I was pleased with my hundred against the MCC because after my failure in Australia I needed to occupy the crease and get runs. At the start I felt ill at ease and I needed to familiarise myself. Then I played a good off-drive against Jon Agnew – I got my foot well across to the pitch of the ball and it screamed through mid–off. It all came together after that and that shot made me feel so much better. Earlier a couple of drives hadn't gone in the right area and I was looking for one good shot off the front foot to get me going. A lot of batting is instinct, what you're taught, but you need a little luck to make it all count. Much is from the head and eyes, and then you have to co-ordinate the feet and hands and work at your timing.

This day it was very cold, but the pads kept me reasonably warm and the cool breeze was welcome. I got dropped on 99 by John Carr at mid-off, an early-season effort by him. The ball pitched right on my foot as it hit the ground and I jabbed it to mid-off. The ball spilled out after Carr hit his knee with his hand, and I escaped. I don't think I've ever been out on 99 in a first-class game. I won't freeze up, I like to get through the nineties as fast as I can. Sometimes I'll tighten up and get there with a few singles but, in those circumstances, I'm always very quick on to the loose ball. Now and then I'll get away with one that goes over the heads of the slips, but that's just being positive. In all my innings I just go out and play and try to remain positive in my approach. Sometimes I'll just lift my bat and look sheepish if I've reached a hundred that contained a few risky shots and some dropped catches but on occasions I'll be really pleased because I've worked for it. Either way, there's always a sense of achievement.

While I was out in the middle, enjoying myself after I'd reached three figures, Beefy was padded up, willing us to stay in. He was in a no-win situation, because we were going to declare soon and if he got out cheaply the press would have been on his back. He also had no time to graft. We were all so short of practice that we had to take any opportunity that came our way and Beefy knew that. I never had any doubt that he'd make it after his back operation; he loves the game too much and he wouldn't have wanted to leave it while still so young. Also he wanted to prove wrong all those who'd written him off – that's his main motivation. Many now say that they expected him to come back but that minimises the extent of his recovery. Just to see the scars on his back and the work he has put in underlines how important it all was to him.

He's now very fit. Since he was suspended in 1986 he has looked at least a stone and a half overweight, but this injury has at least done him some good in that he's now more disciplined in his eating habits. When we were rained off in Singapore and Brisbane, Beefy played a lot of racketball and I was the only one who could claim to be fitter than him. Even then he wouldn't admit that in front of me! I'm lucky because I actually enjoy training with weights in the fresh air and working out at aerobics. In New Zealand I've gone to aerobic classes for the past two winters and now I can touch my toes, something I couldn't do a couple of years ago. My mobility and strength have increased a lot in recent years and yet Beefy, eleven years my senior, can still keep up with me. He is a fantastic competitor.

While Hick reacquainted himself with the middle of the bat in cold, cheerless weather at Lord's, his co-diarist contented himself with a gentle workout and an appreciative study of the young master.

➤ DILLEY:

The feeling is that, if Hicky can play like this without any match practice, what's he going to be like when he's fully acclimatised? Already there's talk of him getting a thousand runs before the end of May – you dismiss that but then think, 'Hang on, he only needs another 800-odd and, the way he's going, he'll do that in four knocks.' That shows our confidence in the man's ability. He plays forward defensively and the ball pings to the boundary: he literally blocks them for four. The heavy bat has a lot to do with it, but the secret is timing.

The rest of the lads played well considering the conditions – the umpires reckoned it could've been 50 for 5 at lunch on the first day – but we were in such bad nick that we were missing the ball by miles. Tim Curtis and Gordon Lord fought it out at the start and that's the hallmark of a good side. Meanwhile Beefy sat padded up for ages, not showing any nerves but clearly feeling the need to be doing something to take his mind off the challenge to come. He tends to be even louder when he's waiting to go into bat. Someone will get a clip round the earhole or whacked on the backside with his bat, he'll go quiet for a bit then hunt out my cigarettes, steal a few of them and then give a few orders to Andy, his personal assistant. In the end he didn't get in and he was happy about that, I think.

I had the full quota of jumpers on when we fielded. It was just too much to expect us to play to our best two days after coming back from Australia; it always takes me a long time to get going after a break and it showed as I bowled too many bad balls. Kim Barnett whacked me around a bit, and Robin Smith looked good. I hope the England selectors are as supportive towards Robin as they were with Mike Gatting, because I think he deserves an extended run. He's got class and guts. I had a good look at some of my rivals for the new ball in the Tests and again I was impressed with the accuracy and hostility of Angus Fraser. David Lawrence was a little wild: the feeling is that he either bowls it too full or too short, a fault he shares with Greg Thomas. If those two got the length right, their natural speed would make them fearsome propositions.

I'm not as fast as those two nowadays and I'd rather be driven than pulled. I want to get batsmen in the half-and-half area, where they're unsure whether to go back or forward. My pace is now about eighty-five per cent of what it was when everything was going well. There's just no point in running in and trying to bowl at the speed of light if you're not putting it in the right place. It may look good to have the wicket-keeper diving around and the batsmen hopping about, but it is a waste of time if the ball is only whacking into the keeper's gloves.

Anyway, I honestly believe that the average county pro plays fast bowling better than they did in the days of Lillee and Thomson. Today all that protective gear for the head, arms and ribs gives them extra confidence and the need for runs right down the order means that almost everyone can keep an end up. You see tail-enders go into the nets now and practise seriously. If the ball is there for the whack, they'll have a go and, with these big bats, they've got a chance of scoring runs. There are very few rabbits in the county game these days – Kevin Jarvis at Gloucestershire and Peter Such at Leicestershire are the only two I'd call rabbits, but even Jarvo once won a game by hitting Sylvester Clarke for four. Today a fast bowler in county cricket has to do much more with the ball, rather than just trying to blast them out. It helps if you have a plan in your mind and the necessary control. I just hope I can regain my control before the season's much older.

Worcestershire began the defence of their championship at Trent Bridge on 20 April, the earliest start in the history of the county championship. The weather remained bitterly cold, with rain a constant threat, and Sunday's Refuge Assurance match was washed out. Yet Worcestershire started the serious part of the season encouragingly, a solid team performance bringing a seven-wicket victory. Dilley picked up welcome wickets (5 for 42 in the first innings, 2 for 40 in the second), while Hick made two half-centuries in the match (56 and 55 not out), the final one a swift affair with one eye on the gathering clouds.

 HICK:

Phil Neale and I just had to get on with it on the final day because the rain was due. I felt we deserved to win. They were trying to bowl us out so they had a few close fielders in round the bat, and that left some open spaces in the field. Although I've got a few runs in each innings it still doesn't feel right. I'm not tight enough, I'm messing around with my grip and I'm not happy with my stance. I have to feel comfortable at the crease but my mind is too preoccupied at the moment. Australia and my lack of match practice in English conditions both dog me. I'll have to make a decision soon on the first one and hope the weather and the wickets improve soon.

I thought Graham bowled very well, considering that there's always a chance of an injury to a fast bowler in these early-season games. From my position at slip he seemed to me to be coming through to the keeper's gloves with a fair degree of pace and he beat the bat a lot. Franklyn Stephenson tried me with the slower ball a few times, the incredibly slow one that got him a lot of victims last year. He hasn't done me with it yet, although a couple of our lads have been trapped. Last year the boot was on the other foot against us and when we got him with the slower one, he turned to us in the slips and gave us a great wide melon smile. He's a lovely fellow.

Eddie Hemmings didn't get much of a bowl because the conditions favoured the seamers but I always enjoy our duels. He's a spinner from the old school: he likes to flight the ball, get the batter down the track and look for a stumping. He can change the flight of the ball from the position he takes at the crease. He either bowls it straight over the top or from an open-chested position. I think John Emburey is just the better off-spinner: he has a lot in his armoury, he's tall, gets bounce and gives you nothing. Perhaps Eddie bowls too straight. I feel an off-spinner should bowl off-stump, or just outside, and look for the turn or bowl the one that floats away from the right-hander, as Embers does. Two fine, experienced bowlers.

Derek Randall held us up in the first innings with a typical knock. He can easily annoy the bowlers because he's always fidgeting at the crease and hits the ball in strange places. Then, after backing away to leg to hit you over cover, he'll settle down and play properly for a time. He doesn't get right to the pitch of the ball – he likes to give himself room to hit it, playing wide of his pad. Because he plays wide of his body, you feel he can get a nick early on, but he has a good eye and times the ball so well. You never really see Randall take a big swing at the ball. He tends to push it and it races away. He always seems to enjoy himself. That tends to annoy the bowlers even more.

Everyone wanted to see Ian Botham in his first championship match since his operation. He didn't bat very well at all – he was trying to hit the ball too hard and it was never there for him. He was getting it on the toe of the bat and the ball was just trickling away. A few snicks and swishes and then a merciful end for him. When he bowled he showed he could still swing it, although he was a little wayward. It was so cold that he relied on the strength of his shoulders to propel the ball, rather than any great body action, and that was sensible. He just ran up rather daintily, put it on the spot rather than really bowled it, and kept muttering on about Tom Cartwright, his mentor early in his career, who bowled in similar fashion. I think Beefy will soon return to his old ways once he is more confident, but for now it's amusing to watch him try to con out the batsmen. He keeps hinting that they were lucky to have got a bat down on the ball in time, that he has them worked out. He takes it as a personal insult when someone whips him away through leg-side if the ball pitches on off-stump, but he conveniently forgets that he plays that shot when it's his turn. All batters hit a ball like that from extra cover through to mid-wicket if their eyes and timing are good enough: the secret is to pick the right length for the shot, rather than the line. If someone does that to Beefy, he winces and curses his luck, and I'm sure many have frozen in the past and buckled under his psychological pressure. It gets the younger ones doubting whether they are in fact playing well, whereas his old mates will just tell him to get back to his mark and get on with the bowling. At the moment he is a yard too slow but he'll be trying to build up his pace so that they can't change their shot once he's beaten them with late swing. He, of course, is sure that will come.

DILLEY:

I don't think I've bowled particularly well in this game but when you're picking up wickets it's a nice consolation. I aimed to bowl for rhythm but I struggled because I was worried about my right knee. I wasn't getting to the wicket in the right position and my arm was a little low. In these overcast conditions, the ball inevitably seamed around and I enjoyed the dismissal of Chris Broad. He left the delivery alone and it clipped his pad, prompting a huge appeal for lbw from yours truly. I couldn't believe he wasn't given out, but then some of the lads rushed up to congratulate me. I'd turned round for the appeal and hadn't noticed that the ball had gone on to the off-stump via his pad.

Randall was just Randall: he always seems to score runs against me. He moves around the crease so much that you tend to bowl at him rather than the stumps, so you send one a foot outside leg-stump when he's hopped over to the other side of the wicket. He hits reasonable balls to amazing places. He chatters a lot to himself and the opposition tend to talk at him to get him going. I don't give out any verbals, other than the occasional 'Bloody hell, this is a great game – nick, four, nick, play and miss, four.' I used to dish it out, but that was frustration born of inexperience. I used to think nobody should hit me for four, I expected a wicket every ball. I still do, but accept it's not going to happen. It's not the batter's fault that he plays and misses, or that the umpire doesn't give him out. It's up to the bowler to put the ball in the right place.

It was difficult to get through the first day, in particular at Trent Bridge. At the start it's okay, because you're fresh and warm, having just come out of the dressing room, and you soon get a sweat on. But the hardest part is coming back for another spell after stiffening up. The wind gets to the joints, the muscles tighten up and it remains like that no matter how much you try to loosen up. You have to take it easy to avoid doing any damage, so you run in gingerly, being extra careful when it's blowing a gale. The batsmen know all of that and they're ready to whack your gentle looseners.

We all burst out laughing at Beefy when he came back to the dressing room after he was out. It was an awful innings, a cameo of its kind, and he knew it and shared the amusement. He smeared one through mid-on to get off the mark as he aimed for mid-off, and came down to the bowler's end grinning all over his face. It was too much to expect him to whack it all over the place so soon after arriving back in England after Australia. He was under great media pressure at Trent Bridge but that doesn't seem to bother him. However, that may just be a case of not allowing the nerves to show.

Franklyn Stephenson took some stick as Hicky and the captain accelerated on the last afternoon. An interesting cricketer, Frankie. I'm very pleased he's done so well after taking so much criticism when he replaced Clive Rice and Richard Hadlee. I remember once Alan Knott told me that no first-class cricketer is a bad cricketer and it was ludicrous to write off Frankie without giving him a full season at Trent Bridge. After all he had been close to the West Indies team before going off on a rebel tour to South Africa, and he proved his ability by doing the 'double' last year. That slower ball of his is fantastic – he really makes the batsman look stupid when it works. He holds the ball in the normal seamer's grip then just as his hands are coming up to deliver it, he slips the ball deeper into his palm. His arm comes over at the same speed, but the ball goes higher and slower. I've been experimenting with that but I haven't yet mastered it, and I don't want to lose my rhythm. A lot of fast bowlers are using the slower one now. I basically have two methods for mine. The first one is easy to pick – I just run up the same and send it down slower. The other one involves bowling a spinner, turning the ball around in my palm as my right arm comes over and using the grip for an off-spinner. That one is going quite well.

Worcestershire travelled back down to London in good heart. An early win in the county championship was important to take the pressure away and it was satisfying to beat a good team that had won the title in 1987, especially as the weather might have ruined the contest on that final afternoon. So to Lord's and a different challenge to the four-day game – the first zonal match in the Benson and Hedges Cup. An early victory in the competition was essential to keep the momentum going and to avoid a dreaded early departure from the competition. Middlesex gave the game to Worcestershire by the narrow margin of one run after they seemed to be in a winning position.

DILLEY:

Because of rain it was touch and go whether we were going to play at all. Phil Neale wanted us to play because there was a chance of getting two points for a win, rather than one for a no-result, and it worked out, thanks to the generosity of Middlesex. We were there for the taking and they blew it: 80 for 3 at one stage, needing just 115 to win and stacks of wickets in hand. Then Beefy got Roland Butcher to smash one to cover-point, something Butcher is always likely to do. Not even Beefy could claim that that dismissal was part of some deep strategy! Then he persuaded Ramprakash to spoon one up to me at mid-off and proceeded to tell us he'd held that one back.

I didn't bowl all that well and helped get them off to a flier. I always find it hard to get into a match when the start has been delayed. I get bored sitting around and then find it hard to concentrate enough when we finally get out on the field. Thank goodness for Beefy's Golden Arm: they often say that a low target is more difficult to chase than a large one because you are tempted to change your normal way of batting, and Beefy cashed in on their uncertainty. He got the Gold Award just for taking three wickets, although the press reacted as if he'd scored a double hundred and taken all ten. It was yet another example of his competitiveness. He refused to believe we were out of it.

I believe he lives off days like this. He needs the publicity that follows. I'm sure he knows a lot more that is printed about him in the tabloids than he'll admit – he'll often say, 'Don't read that, it's all crap,' so he seems to know what the despised papers are writing about him, even though he professes not to read them. He's not stupid, he's aware of his marketability and he wants to live comfortably. Beefy once admitted to me that his earning power really took off after he was banned for smoking cannabis in 1986. That of course shouldn't be the case, but the British public have a love–hate relationship with larger-than-life characters like Ian. I'm envious about what he earns from the game but I just couldn't put up with being analysed so closely. He must be very strong mentally and have a big ego to be able to withstand it all, but he does. Now he's back I'm pleased for him that he's making a contribution to the team. We've missed each other. He got us out of jail in this game and we sat in the dressing room thinking, 'If we can sneak this one, we can win anything.' We're short of runs, but the bowlers are doing it and the fact that we won despite playing badly suggests a great season once the batters come good.

⊖ HICK:

I got out to a leading edge, with the ball holding up off the seam, and that summed up the wicket. It was slow and difficult to score runs freely and Beefy was just the right pace as a bowler. In the end they were scared to get out to him and, after playing out a few tight overs, they bottled it and threw the game away. They thought that all they needed to do was to occupy the crease and with their middle order a little inexperienced the pressure got to them. Butcher's dismissal was very amusing. In the slips I said to our keeper, Steve Rhodes, 'He's going to get out next ball – he'll drive it to Dolly at point,' and sure enough that's exactly what happened. Steve just looked at me and burst out laughing. Sometimes you just feel a dismissal coming on when you're in the slips, especially if the batter's looking edgy. This time I guessed right. Steve occasionally manages a correct forecast about a nick as well!

Afterwards we agreed we'd been lucky but it was vital to get that first win in the qualifying rounds. We're in a tough group and the next stage must be another win, which will leave us just one victory short from the remaining two matches. That would surely get us into the next round.

Next stop, Edgbaston and a four-day fixture against Worcestershire's nearest neighbours, Warwickshire. More cold weather, with squally showers affecting the later stages after the first day had been completely washed out. At least there was an exciting finish in a low-scoring match dominated again by the seamers. Warwickshire needed two to win off the last ball from Richard Illingworth, but Gladstone Small drove it straight back, it hit his partner Geoff Humpage and they could only scramble a single. The scores finished level, but Warwickshire garnered eight more points because they had batted second. The run-chase had been set up by a challenging declaration from Ian Botham, who had taken over the captaincy from Phil Neale, whose bout of glandular fever was expected to keep him out for several weeks. For Graeme Hick it was another disappointing game as he was dismissed twice for single figures. The unreliable pitches were beginning to reduce even Hick to the status of a mere mortal and there was much less talk of a thousand runs by the end of May.

⊖ HICK:

I haven't thrown the idea out of my mind – after all I've now got almost 300 runs before April is out, but I'm not playing well. Last year, the surfaces I batted on were usually good and I was moving my feet well. Now I'm in two minds – whether to go back or forward – and that sums up my uncertainty over the Australian dilemma. I feel confident enough in the nets but taking confidence out into the middle is proving difficult. On tricky surfaces like this Edgbaston one, I've got this fear that I'll play forward and get smacked in the face or on the fingers. I have to get that out of my mind. All of the batters feel the same. Tim Munton got me out twice at Edgbaston – he's a good, accurate seam bowler who knows how to use favourable conditions. In the second innings, the ball kept low and I was so plumb lbw that I almost walked. In the first innings, I was well caught at slip. I asked Damian D'Oliveira what had happened and he said he couldn't work out how I'd nicked it – it was a ball of full length, I went for the off-drive and I got an edge. Annoying. It was a typical early-season English pitch and Gladstone Small and Tim Munton exploited it well, but we were always confident of out-bowling them and so it proved in the first innings. Graham not only hit the seam, but swung it very cleverly. He and Neal Radford were almost unplayable when Warwickshire batted.

Steve Rhodes got us out of trouble in the second innings to set up the declaration. He's a very big asset in the middle order. He's so confident now about his batting, he's very tight and runs brilliantly between the wickets. He sometimes loses confidence when he doesn't get in to bat – last season was an example – but he's going to get plenty of chances to bat if the wickets stay like this for much longer. In the end we were happy to hold on because we didn't play all that well. It was a generous declaration and it needed to be, because you don't often bowl out a county side in less than forty-five overs unless they're going for the runs. They should've won it because the wicket flattened out in that last afternoon. We are still rusty from Australia, but at least we have avoided defeat in our last two games when each time we couldn't have complained about it.

We are going to miss Phil Neale's captaincy. You get into a rhythm in the field with your usual captain, you know where he wants you to stand. Under Beefy we are a little unsure about exactly where he wants us, so that we're drifting a few yards away. Beefy tried really hard as captain, he wanted to do well for everyone. He was more serious than usual in the field, looking around, lost in thought. At the intervals he'd talk to Steve Rhodes about the bowling – a keeper sees such a lot – but he said very little to the rest of us. I got the impression he wasn't as responsive to suggestions as Phil, that he would follow his own instincts more. He automatically has the respect of the players but I think he will try to lead from the front, rather than be too democratic. I'm sure Beefy will feel happier about his own game when he gets some runs. We all hope that will be soon.

It was another successful game for Dilley, six more wickets giving him thirteen in two championship games so far. The selector-nudging had already started, although Dilley was still concerned about his knee. Two other incidents in the Edgbaston game troubled him.

▭━ DILLEY:

I think it's wrong that the regulations meant we got eight points less than Warwickshire, even though we finished on level scores. We contributed just as much to the game, our generous declaration gave both sides a chance. It wasn't our fault that Gladstone Small hit Geoff Humpage's chest, one of the largest targets on the ground. Why should they get twelve points because they won the toss and batted last? They weren't superior to us, and, even though Worcestershire have benefited from it in the past, it's one of cricket's little puzzlers. They failed to score enough runs to win the game, yet they get eight points more.

I got another five-wicket haul in the first innings, but you'd back yourself to do well on a wicket like this one. So much now stems from the experience of Nottinghamshire in 1981, when they won the title on sporting pitches at Trent Bridge. At the time their batters told me that they'd back themselves to get more runs on such surfaces than the opposition because Rice and Hadlee were such good bowlers. More and more counties are following that lead – and Warwickshire, with their group of fine seamers, seem to be one of the recent converts. That's why Hicky is so valuable to us and that's why we struggle when he doesn't get his expected quota of runs, as in this game at Edgbaston.

Statistically I've made an encouraging start and, if the pitches carry on like this one, I'll have a few more. I've never been a prolific wicket-taker at county level, even though my strike rate of wickets to overs is good. Neal Radford will always top me in county terms but I like to think that I've won a few games for Worcestershire in the matches where I have played. I'm not the first strike bowler who plays for England to have his county form levelled against him, nor do I like all the criticism that flies around from those who don't understand the point of having a strike bowler. He's not there to bowl line and length, his job is to get the best batsmen out. An initial burst of 3 for 30 off his eight overs is much better than 0 for 12 any day. Averages don't matter, it's wickets per overs that are the real test. The strike bowler should be good enough to get the class players out by a combination of speed and variety, then have enough stamina to come back at the middle order after lunch, and finally clean up the tail. He needs men round the bat to get the edges and that's when the captain has to forget about the nicks that don't go to hand and end up over the boundary. Other bowlers in the side can make the batsman really work for his runs, but the strike bowler should make them glad to get up the other end away from him.

Phil Neale looks awful. He says he's just knackered all the time and the fact that he's run-down means he's more liable to a blood disorder. He's right to get this cleared up before the season is much older, rather than just hanging on. He's had a traumatic year – his benefit, the strains of winning the championship and, more seriously, his son being struck down with leukaemia. We all hope he's back soon. I have the utmost respect for Phil as a person and captain. To me he *is* Worcester, as important as our secretary Mike Vockins. Phil holds everything together as buffer between players and committee: each group has a different order of priorities, and Phil and Mike oil the wheels. When I first played against him as captain, he wasn't very good at judging his declarations. I remember one game at Hereford when he wouldn't set Kent a target because, after a poor run, there was a danger that Worcestershire might lose again and the members might have a go at the team. But Ian Botham has encouraged him to be more positive, to be prepared to run the risk of losing before you can win.

Phil lets a lot of Beefy's bravado go over his head but he transmits confidence to the rest of the side and sifts through the input. Phil

34

encourages us all to chip in, then makes his own decision. You'll never get complete agreement at a team meeting but I think it's healthy that we're allowed free expression. Phil might think an idea is rubbish, but he wouldn't say so – he must sometimes think he's presiding over a bunch of sixth-formers and it's just as well that he's been a schoolmaster. When Beefy and I signed for Worcestershire we knew that a lot of the things people alleged about us were untrue and Phil was completely open-minded. We had confidence in our own ability and Phil treated us like adults. He is an excellent stabilising influence as captain.

I don't think Beefy should be taking over as captain. His captaincy style wouldn't be mine – there's too much blazing of cannons, rather than regrouping. I didn't particularly enjoy playing under him for England a few years ago, because I was very young and I needed someone I could respect as the captain, rather than being my mate. I admire him greatly as a player and friend, but my choice would be Tim Curtis: he is calm and sensible like Phil, he has the respect of the other players, handles the public relations aspects very well, and he's now used to having confident, positive players around him. This would be an ideal time to give Tim some experience in the job to be ready when Phil packs it in. The role will appeal to Beefy's professional pride, but they could have massaged that just as easily by taking him on one side and saying, 'Look, prove some of those wrong who say that you wouldn't be unselfish enough to help Tim. He will be the long-term captain here and you could do a valuable job by advising him as the stand-in skipper.' I reckon Beefy would respond positively to something along those lines. He is a big enough man and teammate to respond. I shall stay away from Beefy as much as possible when he's captain, I shall bowl when he tells me and avoid rocking the boat by saying my piece. There's no point in speaking my mind on the matter because the die is cast.

As April ended, Graeme Hick made a decision about Australia. He turned down Queensland's offer and resolved to spend the winter in Zimbabwe.

HICK:

Everybody keeps asking me what I'm going to do about Australia and it's all been getting on top of me. Now that I've made up my mind I feel almost light-headed. I haven't been enjoying life like I usually do and now I'm happy the decision has been made. This feeling of uncertainty just wouldn't go away. I rang up Mum and Dad and talked it through with them. I asked our coach Basil D'Oliveira for advice and he said it would do me good just to relax for the winter. I might be restless by Christmas, but I'll be playing some club cricket. I've had a hectic couple of years in which I've come from being an ordinary young county cricketer to someone of whom so much is now expected. It'll be nice to go back and see all my friends, people who have always been supportive. Many of them have promised to be at whatever ground I make my England début on (fingers crossed, of course), and I believe them. My parents live in a place called Trelawney, about fifty miles north of Salisbury. Dad runs a tobacco farm there and we also have five hundred cattle. The next farm is about eight miles away, and the village is just a couple of shops and a garage. Blink and you've missed it. I'm very close to my parents and to my sister and brother-in-law, who're both a few years older than me. My sister always looked after me at school and I'm delighted that she's about to make me an uncle for the first time. My brother-in-law is a splendid chap and I shan't be able to see much of him and the family for the next couple of years if all goes to plan. This winter seems an ideal time just to get back to them and it'll be nice to see the new arrival.

I'm glad all that's been sorted out. Money isn't everything. I hope I will eventually go to Australia and play for a state because the experience will be invaluable. The next priority is playing well and getting some runs.

A RUDE AWAKENING

On the first day of May, Worcestershire's players drove to London for an important one-day game against Surrey at the Oval. It was the first of two remaining matches in their group that would decide if they were to progress to the next round of the Benson and Hedges Cup. At this stage of the season, such games are often a lottery. Luck with the toss and the weather is a crucial ingredient as every side hopes for a morale-boosting start to the assault on four trophies.

DILLEY:

We're in a very hard group but, after beating Middlesex last week, we know what we have to do. We qualify if we beat two out of Surrey, Gloucestershire and the Combined Universities, and if we win all three we get a home draw. The Universities side shouldn't be much of a problem, so at the very least we need one win out of two against the counties. On our day we ought to beat Surrey. We know that Sylvester Clarke will play, but he's not really fit after a cartilage operation, so that's a plus. A few fearsome overs from Sylvers can change any game. They're a young side, in a transitional phase, and man for man there isn't really a contest between the two sides. But they have some underrated players. Chris Bullen is one. He always seems to bowl a good line – around middle and leg at slow medium pace – and he is very difficult to get away. Our batters say they're looking to get after him early to disrupt his line. It's funny how some players like Bullen give the opposition hang-ups. I struggle to bowl at certain players – the Wells brothers at Sussex, Paul Parker, Paul Johnson at Notts – when it all seems to fly out the window. There's no common thread between them, I just worry less at bowling to someone like

Border or Gower. I hope Bullen doesn't perform well again tomorrow, because we really need to win this one to feel confident about qualifying. To be out of one of the four competitions in the first few days of May isn't the best start to anyone's season.

⊝ HICK:

It's nice to settle into my usual routine on away trips. That means rooming with Damian D'Oliveira, something we've done for four years now. We always end up having a few beers and a bite to eat somewhere, relaxing and talking about what's to come. We believe in the same things – play hard on the field and try to relax away from the cricket – and we see a lot of each other on days off. We play golf together and, with my girlfriend Jackie getting on well with Damian's wife Tracy, we enjoy eating out as a foursome. Their two children are fun, too: Marcus, their little boy, is three now, an interesting age. I spend a lot of time throwing a ball at him, just to see if he's got any of his father's talent. Good training now that I'm about to become an uncle! One strange thing about my choice of room-mate: Damian smokes and I hate being in a small room with smoke around. I suffered badly from asthma as a kid and that's the reason why Dad stopped smoking. Being brought up on a farm, I've always enjoyed the fresh air, so I notice how one cigarette lingers in a room for hours. So Damian tries to smoke elsewhere when we're sharing a room.

We shan't underestimate Surrey, because they have some good players. I think Ian Greig is a good captain and a strong-minded one. He's not afraid to rebuild, put his faith in the youngsters and let players go who haven't been great team-men. Alec Stewart is a dangerous batsman but he should make more runs. Maybe he doesn't do himself justice because he also has to keep wicket. That's asking a lot of a top-order batsman. At his age, I don't think you can turn someone into a wicket-keeper. Until this season, Surrey had Jack Richards doing the job and he was an England player only last summer. Now Stewart has had to take over and still score his usual runs. The lads reckon Sylvester Clarke is really struggling now but I'll believe that when I see it. He can still let it go even though he just strolls up to the wicket. I made my championship début against Surrey at the end of the '84 season and I had to face Sylvers, batting at number nine. He came round the wicket at me and really put me through the mincer. I was quite nervous because I had no idea what he was going to bowl and how intimidating he was.

Whatever happens tomorrow, we'll play on a decent wicket. Surrey's groundsman, Harry Brind, has done a great job replacing the square and you can usually expect even bounce and enough encouragement for bowlers and batters. On a good wicket, we have to fancy ourselves.

The match went to the final ball, with Surrey winning by one wicket. Sylvester Clarke slogged Dilley to long-off and he just managed to lumber two runs, beating the throw by inches. Worcestershire's players felt Clarke had failed to beat the throw, but they agreed that Surrey were always marginally ahead of them throughout the match.

DILLEY:

It was a good wicket and we should've got more than 200 on it. But we got a lot closer than I thought at one stage – when they're 120 for 2, chasing 191, there's not a lot you can do, except keep plugging on. We were lucky that Hicky came on to bowl when he did, because Alec Stewart hit him into the building site of the new stand and conveniently lost the ball. Convenient for us – because the replacement swung a lot. No idea why, but we then worked our way back into the game. Graham Clinton, who'd battled away, said to me, 'I'm going to have to slog Both, because I'm not going to get many from your end,' and next thing he's done that and holed out at long-off. We kept a slip in, because it was swinging so much and Beefy took two beauties there. We were back in the game, although we knew we had to bowl them out to win. There weren't enough runs to play with.

By the time I bowled the last over, I was really hyped up. I was in a very good spell and I remember thinking to myself that there weren't many bowlers in the world as good at what I was doing then – swinging the ball late, with no one able to lay a bat on me. Even on the last ball, when they needed only two, I told myself,

'There's no way they're going to do it because I'm better at what I'm trying to do than what Sylvers is trying to do.' The reason why he managed to get two runs was because Damian D'Oliveira was too far out on the long-off boundary and he had to run in to field the ball. He was there to stop the boundary and that was a waste of time.

It's difficult to know who to blame for that – as captain Beefy was responsible for the exact field-placing but he was far away at slip on a big ground and perhaps he thought Dolly was nearer than he in fact was. Beefy was still thinking hard about the game because he told me to bowl short of a length at Clarke. I didn't want to do that, I just wanted to bowl normally – with a bit of luck he would've missed a swinging delivery completely. I didn't want to fire in the predictable yorker, because Sylvers would have been expecting that and he is so strong that he could have mishit the ball for four. It turned out that I was about three inches adrift in my line and he hit it reasonably well on the half-volley. As for Dolly's position – I suppose I should've made sure where he was before I bowled that last ball, but you can't think of everything. All I knew was that I had gone from being the best at what I'm trying to do, to the guy who's lost us the game. The responsibility lay with me, even if they only needed one off my last over.

I couldn't hang around outside the pavilion, waiting for the awards ceremony, and I got to the dressing room as fast as I could. I know that sounds unsporting, but I was upset and wanted to find sanctuary. I made a point of congratulating Ian Greig and the Surrey lads, but mentally I'd given everything I had and I needed some space of my own. I wanted to put a towel over my head, have a smoke and sit with my own thoughts and a drink for a while. A performer is more critical of his work than a spectator and, after a bad day, you have to prepare yourself for re-entry on a public stage. At that time I knew I couldn't face all those requests for autographs if I hung around in public view. Now I know the majority of them are well meaning, but I just cannot understand what credence anyone can put on a scribble on a piece of paper. I only ever asked once for an autograph as a little boy and a certain Kent fast bowler told me to get lost in no uncertain terms. I can understand kids asking for autographs but some who thrust the book at you (at the wrong time) are mature adults. What can it possibly mean to them? I mean, I really like Elton John and I enjoy his company as well, but it would mean no more to me to have his autograph than Joe Smith's. So, after losing the game, I needed to escape to my own mental home in the dressing room before I could face what to me is basically nonsense.

It was a quiet dressing room, to say the least. For a time everyone is alone with their thoughts, wondering where we went wrong and making sure in their own mind they weren't the root cause of the defeat. That was more difficult for me this time. Our chairman Duncan Fearnley and our cricket chairman Mike Jones came in to say, 'Hard luck, lads, never mind.' But players do mind after they've been through a long and mentally tiring day and lost the game off the last ball through our own fault. I had another worry to face: my knee had given out again, and although it wasn't painful, it was still a problem. While running in to bowl, the right knee just collapsed and I had to stop, click it back in and start my run-up again. Sounds painful, but it wasn't. I fear I'm getting near to the surgeon's knife again, though,

By the time we had absorbed the game, the spirits of the lads had risen. The journey back could've been a shocker but we had something to look forward to. We stopped at one of our usual haunts on the way back to Worcester, a great pub called the Crown Inn at Blockley in the Cotswolds. Brilliant food, an assortment of real ales and a lovely place to come to terms with our disappointment. It was way past midnight before any of us got to Worcester but you accept that you have to unwind after a day like this one. Now we have to be positive, to tell ourselves that we nearly beat Surrey even though we didn't play very well. When we do get it right, we are the best team around. We must get it right against Gloucestershire in the next B and H game, otherwise we're out. Does anyone know who plays for the Combined Universities?

HICK:

It may have seemed a nail-biter but they were always ahead of us. Dill wasn't left with enough runs to defend when he started that last over and he did really well to get us so near. It's always worse when you lose off the last ball even when you've pulled it back from certain defeat, but we can't complain, especially after the way Middlesex threw away our first B and H game last week. We could have played two, lost two by now – and there's not much hope of qualification from there.

As a team we didn't bat well – too many got in, then got themselves out – and I wasn't happy with my own effort. Greig had just come on with his medium pace and I felt it was time to go up a gear after settling in. Then I got myself out, caught behind, trying to run it down to third man. Very annoying. I never felt really comfortable. Clarke hit me on the helmet early on and it went over the keeper's head for two byes. That came because I wasn't focusing properly on the ball. I was conscious that I was hanging back too often and missing out on the drive. My footwork wasn't right, I was getting into the wrong positions. I felt I could get runs with the cut, because I had more time for backfoot shots, but I wasn't confident about judging balls of fuller length. I feel I've missed a good chance of battling back to form on a good wicket. I'm not sure how many we'll see that are as good as this one.

Basically they won because Clinton hung around and batted through much of the innings to anchor it. He's very good square of the wicket when it's short and he's defensively tight. If you drift it into him slightly, he'll play you away well off his legs. He performs the same solid role as Tim Curtis does for us; if someone like that can bat through most of your innings, you'll get a decent score.

Things were pretty quiet in our dressing room as we tried to assess the day. But it brightened up when Dill handed a five-pound note over to Paul Pridgeon. Dill was taking his fitness campaign so seriously that he had bet Pridge a fiver that he would stay off beer for a month and drink white wine and soda if he wanted alcohol. They struck the bet just before the Surrey game started – a few hours later, Dill had conceded defeat! I think this time we can all sympathise with Dill's need for a few pints.

A RUDE AWAKENING

As Worcestershire prepared for their first home match of the season – a championship game scheduled for four days against Lancashire – Dilley faced up to a decision he had known was imminent. He was going to play in South Africa. His England career would soon be over.

▭▶ DILLEY:

Ali Bacher, the managing director of the South African Cricket Union, rang me, asked for complete confidence and put the question to me. Without hearing too many details I said yes – I'll go there. I know I'll be banned for seven years but at least we all know where we stand. Graham Gooch and his team didn't expect to get more than a year's ban when they went in 1982, but we can't complain about the penalty. I was always going to go on the next tour and Ali Bacher knew that. He told me a few of the others involved – Chris Broad, John Emburey, Bill Athey – and we were all a little disillusioned with playing for England. I still wanted to perform well for England in this Ashes series, but after ten years of Test cricket it doesn't have the same appeal. I don't get on very well with those who are running the England team.

I'm still very bitter about what happened to Mike Gatting in Pakistan and to me shortly afterwards in New Zealand. I was fined for swearing in frustration at what I thought was another bad umpiring decision – note I didn't swear *at* the umpire – and that was another nail in the coffin. I asked for my passport so I could go home but the management refused. I was so frustrated. That good-conduct bonus of £1000 a man in Pakistan took us all by surprise. We didn't deserve it for a start, because we hadn't been particularly well behaved, even though under great provocation. It seemed to me that Lord's felt we should just get on with it over there, irrespective of the pressure we were under. People keep saying England have won just one Test in recent years but we thought we were being denied the chance by bad umpiring, and nobody in our authority seemed to understand our position. How can they sack Gatt for that barmaid incident after saying they believed his side of the story? If they were going to sack him it should've been for something like the Shakoor Rana incident, rather than anything to do with his private life, and he should've been sacked at the time in Pakistan.

When the news breaks, people will say that I've signed because I'm thirty, with bad knees, but I reckon that if the surgery is successful I could have another two or three years with England. But I would have to play many more years for England to match what I'm going to pick up. The decision isn't a difficult one. Two years ago, I said I'd go on another rebel tour of South Africa and that didn't please them at Lord's. The biggest mistake I've made in cricket was to pull out of the last tour there in '82 because that would have given me security. Instead I lost my England place through injury and then had a year out of the game because of a trapped nerve. I even had to go on the dole. Even if I get forty wickets in this Australian series, I shall still go. Ali wants me and the other guys to do well for England this summer, because, by the time the tour goes ahead, he wants us to be big names to interest the South African public. He was also insistent about secrecy – there is no complete certainty that the tour will go ahead, so any gossiping will only complicate things. That's no problem to me, I can keep a secret. I just hope some of the other lads who get on better with the media than me will keep quiet.

I shall feel a little dishonest about taking Test-match fees this summer while knowing my England career is about to end, but I would be blowing the whistle on Ali Bacher if I asked to stand down from the Test series and I respect him too much for that. We'll all have to keep our heads down for a few months. For the moment, I'm waiting for my contract to come from South Africa.

While Dilley wondered who else would be travelling to South Africa with him, he returned his thoughts to the visit to New Road of the strong Lancashire side. They were among the teams most fancied to take the title away from Worcestershire and over the next few days they looked an impressive unit. In the championship game, Lancashire won with a day and a bit to spare, and they followed that up with a comfortable victory in the Refuge Assurance League. It was hot and sunny at last, but neither New Road wicket favoured batsmen. For Graeme Hick, the lean spell continued.

⊝ HICK:

In the first innings, Wasim Akram moved one in on me and trapped me lbw for 4 runs. He comes on to you quicker than you think because he has a fast arm action. Then, on the Saturday morning, when we really needed a big innings from someone, I was caught at bat/pad by David Hughes when Phil DeFreitas managed to get some extra bounce and I couldn't keep it down. Next day, DeFreitas did me again in the Sunday League, bowling me off my pads as I tried to hit him through mid-wicket. I'm just like all of our batters at the moment – we don't know what's going to happen when we go out there. We're waiting for one to kick even when the pitch goes through a quiet period, and there's no doubt that Lancashire approached both these matches in a more positive frame of mind. People are beginning to talk about the Reader ball now. The feeling is that the prominent stitches on a Reader are favouring the seamers, compared to the Tworts ball, but I don't want to get involved in things like that. If you're concerned about the type of ball that's being used, you're playing into the hands of the bowlers.

We've been a bit defeatist in these two games. When the batsmen are crossing at the fall of a wicket, they're saying, 'It's back to normal, it's doing everything out there,' and that's no way to approach the game. We're walking out without a clue and we're putting ourselves in that position by going on about it. We must put it out of our minds, like Lancashire did. Every one of their players in the championship game had scored a first-class century and they applied themselves. In both innings, their tail-enders added precious runs and we only looked like getting near to the final total on the final afternoon when Dolly and Steve Rhodes batted aggressively. I thought Dolly played really well – playing the ball very late and timing it sweetly. He's the only one to show any consistency at the moment. It was a big game, this four-day one. We knew that Lancashire would be a threat this season and this win will do them a lot of good. It's a blow to lose so badly this early.

Already we're missing Phil Neale's captaincy. Beefy isn't the same person when he's captain out on the field: he's not following the advice he gives to Phil and, instead of taking things calmly and backing a hunch, he's running around all over the place, too keyed up. DeFreitas did him twice in a row for nought after really putting him through it and when he came back to the dressing room he said, 'How the hell can you play that?' That's not what the next man in wants to hear. The frame of mind is very important at times like this and Beefy needs to be his usual bubbly self to help us.

The ball is now bouncing more as the weather improves and that only underlines the variable bounce on our wickets – but we must be more positive, because we have some important games to come at New Road. We shall have to learn from the confident approach of the Lancashire lads, otherwise we'll be out of the Bensons in a few days.

Dilley's start to the season was proving more successful than that of Hick. Another seven wickets in the Lancashire match meant he had taken twenty in the season's first three championship games. He had reached a smooth bowling rhythm earlier than normal and the late swing was controlled. He was looking England's best bowler, certain to trouble the Australians when the Test series began in a month's time. Yet that troublesome knee was to interrupt his impressive progress.

⊂══▶ DILLEY:

We can't delay it any longer, so it's back to the operating theatre for another clean-up. I can't get through an entire season without another operation, so we've chosen a time when there isn't a great deal of cricket. I'll have it after our next Bensons game on Tuesday, hope that we get through and that I'm fit for the next round in a month. It's got to the stage where I have to have it done, otherwise it would be my last season of first-class cricket. I don't want to have an operation, because you never know what might happen, but it's the sensible thing to do.

It's frustrating because I feel I'm bowling well at the moment. Already I'm not far short of the total of wickets I took for Worcestershire last season! Our batters started saying this was a terror track, but once you got over the new ball it wasn't all that bad. At this stage of the season, there's a lot more moisture around early in the day compared to July, so the ball's likely to do more, but people are going overboard, blaming it on the extra stitches on the Reader ball. I'm more philosophical about these things. You should go out on a cricket field determined to do your best and, if that's not good enough on the day, there's not an awful lot you can do.

Lancashire outplayed us, but I'm still not sure that they'll win the championship. They're still a player or two short, I reckon. Phil DeFreitas looked sharp, though. His move from Leicester seems to have worked the trick for him, because he ran in and got plenty of bounce. He really enjoyed working Beefy over two days in a row. I think he's talented but, unless he works at his batting, he's going to be a bowling all-rounder. Someone has to get hold of him and tell him that not every ball has to be whipped through mid-wicket. A couple of bad years at Leicester knocked the confidence out of him, and Micky Stewart has got on at him about having a low arm when he bowls. Yet he makes the ball bounce, even on flat wickets, so not everything has to be approved by the MCC coaching manual. Phil has already been labelled as just a one-day international player and, although that's a little unfair, his Test record is appalling for someone of his ability. He's got to learn to make the ball leave the bat, either through the air or off the seam. If I have learned to do it, so should he. Bob Woolmer, one of the best fast-bowling coaches I've met, used to say swing bowling was all about getting your wrist behind the ball to point down the pitch. If you do that, it doesn't matter if your head's three feet to the left, and stuff what the commentators say about your poor technique. When DeFreitas gets tired, he tends to drop his head to make way for the arm to come swishing through for a fast delivery. If you drop your head, there is more chance that the wrist will follow. But look at Phil Newport, our swing bowler – he's a natural because even though his action is ungainly and open-chested, he keeps his wrist up behind the ball to make it swing.

Lancashire have a good opening pair in Mendis and Fowler and I was pleased to get Mendis first ball, playing down the wrong line. He played very well in the second innings, though. There's talk of him playing for England and, although he does play the quicks well and he has a consistent record, I can't see it. That's not based on his ability – more that he never seems to get in; perhaps his face doesn't fit. Now I don't think that should be a factor in selection, because you should pick the best available players, regardless of personalities. Yet Mendis never gets a chance. Wasim Akram is a talented all-rounder, although I've seen him play some dreadful innings where he can't locate the ball. But he's a dangerous hitter and can turn a game. As a bowler he's learned a lot from Imran – not least how to make a ball swing as if it's new when it's soft and sixty overs old. These Pakistanis have a knack for that.

Jack Simmons played, and although it's always good to see him I wonder what he was doing in a game where there wasn't one over of spin. I admire him for hanging on so long, so near to his fiftieth birthday. They wouldn't have kept on picking him unless he was doing so well in one-day cricket. It must be so difficult to time your retirement right. Jack really loves everything connected with cricket, whereas there are many hassles I don't like about it. Once they start to take too much of my enjoyment from me, I'll pack up. It doesn't matter if it's next week or in six years' time. I just want to enjoy my cricket and not be bothered with the trappings around it.

Talking of Jack Simmons, I heard a lovely story about him from Graeme Fowler. Jack is about the slowest mover in the game now and, when he was running after the ball, a bloke in the crowd shouted out, 'Hey, Simmons, get the ball in, you big fat lump!' Jack got to the ball, turned round at the crowd and shouted, 'Who the —— hell are you, calling me fat?' By now all his team-mates were shouting, 'For God's sake, Jack – get the ball in, they're running!' Someone had to run up and take the ball off him before the batsmen stopped running!

I suppose the major consolations for us were the form of Damian D'Oliveira and Steve Rhodes, bearing in mind that all I did was settle for being boring, try to get the ball in the right place and hope the pitch would help me. But Dolly is now really applying himself. He's been under a lot of pressure after two lean years and, when David Leatherdale replaced him on the morning of the NatWest Final last September, the warning was there. Dolly has obviously told himself that the only way he can hold on to the number-four spot is to stay there, and make a lot of runs. In this game, he got his first championship half-century for two years and, although he ran himself out, it was a fine knock. Steve Rhodes again showed he can score runs and he's keeping brilliantly, standing up to the medium pace of Martin Weston and Ian Botham. He looked terrific on that short tour to Singapore and Brisbane, and he's just carried on the same way. I reckon he's got to be in England's one-day international squad. He'll have to wait another fortnight to know.

Looking on the bright side, at least we had them a little worried on the Saturday afternoon when Rhodes and D'Oliveira were playing so well together. We're also too good a side to be bowled out twice for less than 200. If you start doubting yourselves at the beginning of May, then you've got little chance of winning anything. It'll come right at some stage if you keep going. It's been a bad weekend and we didn't even have the consolation of a win in the Sunday League. So we haven't got going yet and we need to get on a roll in the Sunday games before we get too far adrift. We are champions of that as well, after all. Even though the Sunday stuff is 'formula cricket', we're missing Phil Neale on that day just as much as on others. He still looks pretty awful, though. He won't be back for the Bensons – so that puts even more pressure on Beefy.

Soon it was **Wednesday, 10 May** – and Worcestershire's most important game so far this season. They had to beat Gloucestershire at home to stay in the Benson and Hedges Cup but, in front of a large crowd, they lost by 45 runs. For the second season in a row, the county champions faced early elimination in the B and H. For Graeme Hick, dismissed for 16, that 173 not out at Lord's now seemed an eternity ago. Dilley took 2 wickets for 40 runs.

◯ HICK:

We've blown it and it's our own fault. A team of our ability should get 201 off fifty-five overs, whatever the state of the pitch, but the batters are having a terrible time. We just don't seem to believe we can do it, and no one apart from Dolly looks secure. I was caught at slip off Kevin Curran, playing a nothing sort of stroke. Beefy battled away for a long time, but then got done by Vibert Greene's slower ball, and no one else threatened a big score. We can't blame our bowlers – now and then one of them may have a bad game but we have enough options to make sure we don't get hammered. We've got to get some runs too and stop worrying about these wickets. Our supporters are getting a bit uptight about our results. The members know their game and they come along to see good cricket, with plenty of runs. Our crowds are excellent, the weather is perfect but the entertainment is poor. Our physio, Dave Roberts, seems busy, tending to rapped knuckles and bruised fingers, and the seamers are having a great time. Yet last season, if the opposition got 200, we would have expected to get 201 to win, whatever the circumstances. That's what confidence does for a team. Now we fear the worst and we don't look like county champions.

I need to get my game into some sort of order because my footwork isn't good, I'm getting into no-man's-land at the crease and I'm not reacting positively. Perhaps the Combined Universities bowlers will be more obliging than Gloucestershire's. The Aussies are here this weekend and I'd like to play well against them after my failures last month in Brisbane and the collapse of my deal with Queensland.

Kevin Curran won the Gold Award in this game and we could do with some of his aggression and arrogance at the moment. If he's in the right frame of mind, he's a great competitor. So much depends on his mood, though. If he's had an argument in the dressing room that can fire him up, but if he's worried about his back, he'll decide he doesn't want to bowl. He certainly believes in himself and doesn't seem to have a very high regard for anyone else's ability. Having played with or against him so often in Zimbabwe, players often ask me how to handle him – especially

David Graveney when he was Gloucestershire's captain and he couldn't get Curran to bowl for him. Well, in the Zimbabwe side we used to suggest that a dollar per wicket or run might be a useful way to motivate him! But at the moment I envy him. He and his side are playing with confidence and, unlike us, they can still dream of getting to the B and H Final at Lord's.

DILLEY:

My last game before the knee operation wasn't exactly memorable for us. I don't think the wicket was as bad as some of our lads suggested and they are definitely in danger of getting a complex about it. It was worrying Beefy and he was also uptight about losing every game so far in which he's been captain. I talked to him about his own form and suggested more time at the nets might help. As usual he wouldn't have it, though – he thinks he can just blaze his way out of a bad trot. His bowling is okay, though. It's disappointing to see him running in off just ten paces, but it's his body and he knows what he's doing. It's not as if anyone is whacking him around.

Hicky is going through a phase where his confidence is suffering because he seems to expect to get one that'll scuttle along and hit the base of the stumps. The mere fact that he expects something like that means he's thinking negatively. He's practising hard in the nets, trying to get fully forward or back all the way, because he's getting caught in that half-and-half position. So he's still in danger of getting out to a poor stroke because his footwork is a little static at the moment. I can understand Beefy's positive attitude to batting on these pitches. He thinks he'll get sawn off eventually so he may as well have a great wind-up at anything that's wide of the stumps. If he nicks it hard, it'll be a snorter of a catch. Trouble is, that approach isn't working – otherwise he'd have scored a lot more by now.

I'm not worried about Graeme's run of poor form. He's a little down, but he's still working hard at his game. We all have great faith in his ability and know he'll get it right soon. At the moment it's a pretty quiet dressing room – we've got little to rave about. We're also lucky with our members. After a blow like this one, I can think of a few county sides who would skulk away to a nearby pub to avoid too much earbashing from the members. But ours are pretty understanding. We went into the members' bar and, after a few mumbled words, they left us alone. They could tell we were all pretty pissed off and nobody tried to pump us for post-mortems.

Next day Dilley checked into the Nuffield Hospital in Birmingham for his second knee operation in less than nine months. It was successful. The surgeon expected him to be fit for first-class cricket in a month's time – provided he worked hard in training.

DILLEY:

It was exactly the same operation as last September. When a bit of bone flakes off, it sometimes floats down the cartilage, nicks it and then through wear and tear that piece of cartilage will break off. That floating bit of cartilage is the problem, so they clean it up. I've got used to hospitals after all those tests in '84 for what proved to be a trapped nerve in my spinal cord. At one stage they were checking me out for cancer of the spine or multiple sclerosis, so a knee operation is comparatively mundane after something like that. That was the most worrying period of my life – apart from the time when Michael Holding bowled very rapidly at me in Kingston! Anyway, I now know what I must do if I'm to get back into the England side, and also ensure I'm fit enough for the South African tour. I've got to train hard, cast aside my usual laziness and forget about beer. More white wine and soda!

The following morning, Dilley was discharged and was driven to New Road to watch Worcestershire lose their fifth match in a row and third in succession in the Benson and Hedges Cup. Defeat by five wickets with eleven balls to spare by the Combined Universities was the season's biggest story so far, and Ian Botham's dismissal for nought only added to the spice. Hick's 109 off 123 balls was a consolation as he tried to grope for some semblance of form, but the day belonged to the talented undergraduates.

HICK:

We won the toss and had to bat first because there was the faintest chance of qualifying if we managed to score more than 250 and bowl them out, and if the other games in the group went a certain way. In fact there wasn't even a hope of us getting 250. Chris Tolley, who will be rejoining our staff later in the summer, conceded very few runs at the start of the innings and we were soon struggling. We kept thinking that the next bowling change would bring some runs but they all kept at us. They had nothing to lose. Mike Atherton looked as if he knew how to captain a side and they played a very good game of cricket. At lunch I was still there and hoping for some sort of launching pad, but in the afternoon wickets kept falling. Beefy chased a wide one without getting his foot anywhere near the pitch of the ball and the rest were too tense. The Universities knew they didn't need to bounce us out and bowled sensibly – line and length. In the end I had to stay in and use up all the overs, and if it hadn't been for some good slogging by Neal Radford, it would've been even more embarrassing.

It was a slow wicket and we thought that if we had found it difficult to score freely, then it would've been even worse for them. We were wrong: we were too complacent and didn't bowl at all well. After getting an early wicket, we sat back and thought we would stroll it. At tea-time they were looking good and I walked over to Dolly and said, 'We're nowhere near winning this.' Nasser Hussain came in and played very freely. He played against us last year and I think he'll be an effective one-day player because he likes to play his shots. They won easily. They bowled better, fielded better and approached the target very calmly. Almost all their batsmen chipped in, whereas our innings had a lopsided look. Without that late slog from Radders, the game might have been finished after thirty-five overs!

This wasn't the performance of county champions and the mood in the dressing room afterwards reflected that. We had been badly beaten by eleven lads at universities up and down the country – talented players, but inexperienced and surely no match for us. We couldn't even get a consolation victory after being eliminated from the Bensons. Beefy was disappointed with the match, as captain and player. We desperately need Phil Neale. In the dressing room we tried to talk it out for a while, but it got to the stage where the bowlers were saying, 'Well, we've done our job' and the batters would blame the wicket. Even though you work as a unit, there's a tendency to take sides if you're failing consistently. And we are – that's five defeats in a row. There's no way we should be losing games like this one today. Now we feel alone.

The bar wasn't very crowded by the time we got there, and that accentuated the feeling of being alone. Friends and supporters who are always there when you've done well are nowhere to be seen, the press box is fairly empty (not even they could've expected this defeat!), and you feel you've got to get away. After a spell of teasing our groundsman Roy McLaren, it's suddenly become a little strained between him and the players. We know he's trying to produce the best wicket and it's not working out exactly as he wants, and perhaps we're looking for scapegoats. I don't know much about grounds-manship – few players do – but the feeling is that the dry winter means the wicket hasn't had the normal silt that falls on it when the Severn overflows and floods the ground. So the surface isn't bound tightly together. We're not necessarily blaming the groundsman, but we're hacked off with playing on substandard pitches here. Even though I got a hundred today, it hasn't given me much hope of returning to form. I feel I'm going to get out, I'm not in command. And the Australians are here in a couple of days. I wonder what sort of wicket we'll have for that game?

⊂▬▬ DILLEY:

It was painful enough having to walk on to the ground without crutches, but it was even worse having to watch this performance. The surgeon wants me to start moving around as quickly as I can to build up strength in my knee, so there I was, taking one step at a time, wincing as another one of our wickets fell. There's not a lot you can say to the lads when they've copped a day like that. You've been in the same situation yourself, you know that the press will love the story and you know that five defeats in a row under Beefy's captaincy will be another juicy bone for them.

Already I feel a little like an outsider because you have to be out there on the day to appreciate exactly what's going on, but it seems to me that a lack of confidence is our problem. We're also not pulling together and it gives me no pleasure to repeat how much we're missing Phil Neale. It's proving a nightmare for Beefy: he's finding it hard as captain and he's building up no sort of form with the one-day internationals not far off. He'll be desperate for a good performance against the Aussies.

Heaven knows where we would've been today without Hicky's hundred, but it wasn't vintage stuff and he's getting dragged down by all the uncertainties. But we must remember that the champion county doesn't suddenly become a poor side after a month of the new season. Also give some credit to the university lads. Most of them are on county staffs and later in the summer we'll come up against them in championship games and they'll probably do very well. Atherton clearly knows what he's up to as captain and batter, and John Lever had already told me how highly Essex rate Nasser Hussain.

Worcestershire *v.* Combined Universities
at New Road, Worcester on Thursday 11 May 1989
Combined Universities won by 5 wickets

Worcestershire

1. T. S. CURTIS	b B. HANSFORD	9
2. G. J. LORD	c O'GORMAN b DALE	18
3. G. A. HICK	c O'GORMAN b HANSFORD	109
4. D. B. D'OLIVEIRA	c SPEIGHT b DALE	15
5. I. T. BOTHAM	c SPEIGHT b DALE	0
6. S. J. O'SHAUGHNESSY	c CRAWLEY b BOILING	14
7. S. J. RHODES	c & b CRAWLEY	1
8. P. J. NEWPORT	c DALE b CRAWLEY	1
9. N. V. RADFORD	not out	39
10. R. K. ILLINGWORTH	not out	1
11. A. PRIDGEON		
Extras		9
	Total	216–8

Fall of wickets
1–14 2–48 3–74 4–82 5–116 6–126 7–137

Bowling	O	M	R	W
HANSFORD	11	3	39	2
TOLLEY	11	4	32	0
CRAWLEY	11	1	72	2
DALE	11	2	35	3
BOILING	11	1	32	1

Combined Universities

1. J. J. O'GORMAN	lbw RADFORD	0
2. M. P. SPEIGHT	b RADFORD	29
3. M. A. ATHERTON	st RHODES b ILLINGWORTH	20
4. N. HUSSAIN	b RADFORD	67
5. S. P. JAMES	b RADFORD	65
6. J. I. LONGLEY	not out	14
7. M. A. CRAWLEY	not out	8
8. A. DALE		
9. C. M. TOLLEY		
10. A. HANSFORD		
11. J. BOILING		
T. J. O'GORMAN		
Extras		14
	Total	217–5

Fall of wickets
1–2 2–46 3–152 4–195 5–196

Bowling	O	M	R	W
RADFORD	11	0	38	3
PRIDGEON	9.1	0	41	0
NEWPORT	9	0	46	0
ILLINGWORTH	11	2	29	1
BOTHAM	5	0	25	0
HICK	8	0	35	0

Dilley limped to the home dressing room two days later to watch the first day of the game against Australia. It proved eventful, with twenty wickets falling on that first day alone. The game was over halfway through the second day, with Worcestershire winning by three wickets. It was a farce and Australia refused to play another game on the allotted final day because they felt the wickets at New Road were too unreliable. Only two players gained any satisfaction from the match – Phil Newport took eleven wickets with accomplished swing bowling and Ian Botham, with scores of 39 and 42, showed that the sight of the green Aussie cap could still stir him. Graeme Hick scored 13 and 43.

⊘ HICK:

Beefy played more confidently in these two innings than he has done so far this season. Right from the start he had a go if the ball was there for the drive. When he came in to bat, the atmosphere changed and you could see that the Aussies still saw him as a threat. It was very important to Beefy that we should win a game under his leadership and that he should do well against them. I've always felt the selectors would pick him for the one-dayers on reputation and now that he's done well in this game, he's a certainty.

As for the match itself, it was again a lottery. I didn't feel a great deal of pleasure out of beating the Aussies, because the wicket meant the result could go either way. Their seam bowlers were just feeling their way into the tour and didn't really stretch themselves. Alderman bowled straight, but he always does. As long as you keep your legs out of the way and go forward, he shouldn't be a great danger to England. Lawson swung the ball a fair amount. They weren't happy at all in the whole game. They kept going on about the pitch and were clearly worried about injuries. The wicket was livelier than in the two recent Bensons games here, so the uneven bounce and sideways movement were even more exaggerated. Hopeless for batsmen. Only Border looked comfortable. He played brilliantly in their second innings and didn't play one bad shot until he got out.

Although the pitch favoured the bowlers far too much, you could still appreciate Phil Newport's skilful swing bowling. He can produce a ball that will get anyone out because he's a natural swing bowler. He is very chest-on when he delivers the ball, but his arm comes over straight and he releases the ball at the right moment, with the wrist cocked. Over the last few years Newps has turned good batsmen inside out with deliveries that have swung late when they're expecting it to come back off the seam because of his chest-on action. He used to be simply an inswing bowler who also cut it back off the seam, but one day he took a box of balls and went over to the nets to sort out his technique. He found the right grip for the outswinger and simply taught himself how to move the ball away from the bat.

He's very single-minded in his approach to the game, and as soon as he walks on to the field he changes from an easy-going guy to a hard competitor. Pre-season he'll bowl and bowl in the nets – he knows that with his action he has to make sure everything is right before he can be sure he can still swing it. With a better action, it would simply be a case of fine tuning. He's got more confident about his ability and he's quickened up, while still being able to swing the ball. It's best to bring him on after about twelve overs, when the ball's shine is not so pronounced and he can grip the ball properly. Then he'll bowl you up to fifteen overs on the trot. Often he picks up wickets when not bowling all that well, because when he's got it right he does too much with the ball and the batter isn't good enough to get a touch. The way he's started this season, Newps is on course for a hundred wickets. He must play for England – the Aussies won't be happy with that class of swing bowling. They'll struggle against a bowling line-up of Dilley, Foster, Newport and Fraser.

DILLEY:

From what I saw in this game, I'm more convinced than ever that England will beat Australia in the Test series. The Australians don't like swing bowling. The left-handers, Taylor and Border, are definite candidates for lbw because they leave a gap and play away from their bodies. Boon and Jones play across the line, trying to whip you through mid-wicket. Waugh doesn't like the short stuff. Phil Newport will clean up against them in the Tests and I hope I'm soon fit enough to get at them because I believe I can get a few wickets. As for their bowlers, I reckon Lawson is now past it and I'm not sure if Hughes has got it in him. He'll huff and puff, but after an hour, when the ball has got a little soft, he can be smacked around. I think it will be a high-scoring series, unless we can get the right bowling line-up and swing it enough. Terry Alderman will be treated with respect, even though he lacks that nip he had before his shoulder injury a few years back. He's a lovely chap – we played at Kent together – and he's got a terrific cricket brain. In one county game, he asked short square leg to move to backward short square leg – it was only a matter of a few yards and a thirty-degree angle. Next over the batter played an inswinger straight to the new position and out he went. It looked impressive, even if it was a fluke. Never happens to me!

It was good to have a chat with Terry and the other Aussies – they're a friendly lot. They'll still play it hard on the field, but then have a laugh with you afterwards, unlike the Lillee/Chappell lot I first played against ten years ago. I've never seen the point of behaving like that when the game is over – it's not that important. Meeting up again with Border and the rest has made me really want to get back quickly from my operation. I want to do well this series, if it is to be my last. I'll surprise our lads with the way I get stuck into the training. Dave Roberts doesn't know it yet, but I shall do everything he says. My approach to training is widely known – I've never been one to peak too early! – but I'm looking to lose a stone. There's no chance of the First Test in a month but if I'm lucky I might be on the road back for Worcestershire by then, and then it's the Lord's Test a fortnight later.

While Dilley was vowing to surprise his team-mates, Hick was getting more and more depressed about his form. A year earlier he had been on course for a thousand runs in May and the memory of that remarkable 405 not out at Taunton was still fresh. Now a total of just one century in nine first-class innings was occupying the attention of the cricket media, Worcestershire's supporters and the batsman concerned. He sought out the county's coach, Basil D'Oliveira, for advice.

HICK:

Basil told me to keep my mind fixed on the future, on what I would score by the end of the next day. He said there was just no point in looking back at recent failures, because they would become too important in my own mind – and in any case they couldn't be altered, it was down there in the scorebook. Never forget it was a long season, he told me. Basil knows all about challenges and I really respect him for what he achieved in English cricket after coming over from Cape Town when he wasn't exactly young. Ever since I've been on the staff, I've always wanted to pull out something extra for the coach, and any praise I get from him means a lot to me. Clearly he thinks I've got nothing to worry about but you can't be the same person when you're doing badly. It's your job after all. A lot of people pay to watch us do our job and it's up to all of us to do it as well as we can. I'm a bit quiet at home at the moment and Jackie and I aren't going out all that much. I'm brooding in front of the TV instead. It seems a long time since the lads were talking about another thousand runs in May!

Can I use the wickets at Worcester as an excuse? I haven't exactly done all that well away from home, have I? But my batting is being affected by the New Road pitches and, wherever we play, I'm not going out to bat in the right frame of mind. I'm delaying my entrance out to the middle, whereas I'm normally up and out of the gate as soon as a wicket falls, and the incoming batsman and I always cross on the field. There's talk about me dropping down the order but I honestly feel I've got a better chance early on. When the effect of the roller starts to wear off after an hour, the ball starts doing all sorts of things. The most annoying thing is that those who're running through our batting aren't exactly good bowlers.

The defeatist mood is contagious – we'd watch the play in the dressing room and as soon as we thought a ball had misbehaved someone would say, 'Here we go again!' That's no way to play professional cricket. We must stop moaning about the wickets, but we also hope that the groundsman works the trick soon. We've got a week off now, a week in which I shall work hard in the nets, particularly on my footwork – but we then come back to a Sunday league game and a county match, both at home. Unless we sort ourselves out soon, we're going to get left behind in the championship and the Refuge – and we won both last year.

Meanwhile Dilley was beginning to realise that his verbal commitment to South Africa was leading to a conflict of interest and loyalty. By the middle of May, the Test and County Cricket Board had picked up whispers that Ali Bacher had been active. Players who might be seen as England certainties for the forthcoming series were being asked pointed questions.

DILLEY:

Micky Stewart, England's manager, rang me up and asked if I'd signed a contract to go to South Africa. He didn't ask if I'd been approached, so I could answer that I hadn't signed. Economical with the truth, you might say. I was simply waiting to see the contract before signing it. It seemed odd that Micky didn't press me about my intentions, because I had gone public about South Africa a couple of years ago. There was a twinge of conscience, but it was an honest answer to a question. I didn't want the tour to be called off because it was my benefit, if you like. I'd left Kent before I qualified for one (ten years since you were first capped is the customary time-span), and there was no chance of me playing long enough at Worcester to qualify. I'm just going to sit back, wait for the contract and hope the others keep quiet as well. I'm sure every dressing room around the country is having the same conversation as ours. When it crops up, I simply say, 'I'd like to go if asked and the offer is right.' There's no point in saying anything more at this stage. I'm going and I'm sure the offer will be satisfactory when it arrives.

SEARCHING FOR FITNESS AND FORM

The rest of May was to prove challenging for both Hick and Dilley – Hick as he practised hard in the nets and groped for some semblance of his usual form out in the middle, and Dilley as he tried to get match fit after his knee operation. Dilley's target was twofold: to help Worcestershire recover from a bad start to the season and then to regain his England place.

DILLEY:

I've never worked harder and, believe it or not, I've actually enjoyed it. With a whole week off for the first team, I've been able to provide a variation from the monotony of nets by entertaining them. After our physio, Dave Roberts, works on my knee on the treatment table he takes me out in the sunshine and drives me hard in front of the lads. I've built up from twenty minutes' hard training a day to two lots of forty-five minutes. I train in the morning, go home and then pitch up again in the afternoon to break the day up. Bloody sit-ups, bloody press-ups. When I say to Robbo, 'I'm not very good at these press-ups,' he'll say, 'Right, you do more for saying that.' I soon realised you don't moan with Robbo around, you just get on with it. He knows his job better than I do, it's all down to trust. The flexibility and mobility stuff is important and I've got to make sure I don't lose too much strength in the quadriceps, at the front of the thigh – they must be strong to get me through all that running up to the crease. I've also to remember that I've got another leg and a perfectly good one it is too, but I must work on that one as well so that it doesn't get weaker. After about ten days I find I'm handling the challenge of getting fitter. I can now do a hundred sit-ups without a break.

I've lost a stone. I haven't had a pint for ages, it seems. White wine and soda if anything. We're looking at four to five weeks before I can play first-team cricket again. I mustn't con myself: I have to be sure I can do it out there for the side. England considerations will come later – my first priority is Worcestershire.

HICK:

Dill's been a real eye-opener in his training, because he'd admit he's never been a great one for all that running and stretching. Given half a chance he'd settle for a fag and a game of cards. But he's still training long after he needs to. The lads reckon he's got a double – this isn't really Graham Dilley, is it? He's trimmed right down and looks really fit. Obviously this season means a lot to him.

Cup Final Saturday (20 May). This is something I always enjoy, particularly as my team, Liverpool, is playing. I normally don't get the chance to watch the game live, but with a gap in the fixture list, I can put my feet up and roar Liverpool on. My brother-in-law Mike put me on to Liverpool – I've gone to see them twice over here and each time they lost. They did it today, though. Jackie laughed her head off when Everton got a last-minute equaliser and when Rush got the winner in extra time I was up on my feet, screaming and shouting. That Steve McMahon is some player – he always seems to win the fifty–fifty ball. I could never be as hard as him if I'd played football – you really have to be competitive.

Next day, Worcestershire returned to first-team action and their bad run continued. They lost at home to Surrey by five wickets. So last season's Sunday League champions had started their title defence with two defeats and an abandonment in the first three games. On the same day, England's squad for the one-day internationals was announced and Ian Botham and Steve Rhodes were picked.

HICK:

Phil Neale was back to captain us against Surrey, but it wasn't one of his better days. He dropped himself down to number seven when the slog was on and promoted Steve O'Shaughnessy to five. It didn't work. The captain's a much better player than Steve and, more often than not, you ought to rely on your best batters. Chris Bullen again bowled well against us, coming on at that stage of the innings when the batters are looking to step up the rate. He seems to have us taped. I got 1. My timing was still out and I wasn't playing as straight as I should. Another bad day. At this stage in the development of the side we should be going out there expecting to win and only accepting defeat when we've been going all out for victory. Although we lost by only five runs today, we know the margin flattered us and we should've done much better. If it hadn't been for Dolly's 91 not out, we would've had no chance. He's the only one of us who looks at all comfortable with the bat at the moment.

I was sure Beefy was going to get picked for the one-dayers. When I batted with him against the Aussies last week you could see they were still worried about him and he's been picked on potential. He's England's wild card. We said, 'Well done,' but he wasn't particularly surprised – he clearly expected it. He'd told us he'd be picked all along. I was really pleased for Steve Rhodes. We lived together for two years. He was the tidy one. I kept quiet about the fact that I'm quite a good cook, even though we've always had servants at home. It doesn't do to tie yourself to the kitchen when there's golf to watch on the telly! I think keeping wicket is very hard, especially as they're now also expected to get runs as well. Whenever I take the gloves in a practice session, I really struggle because I'm put off by the bat flashing around near my face when I stand up to the stumps. Steve is very good at spotting things and passing on tips to the captain. Although young, he's played a lot of cricket. His dad used to play for Nottinghamshire and they talk a lot about the game.

DILLEY:

I don't think Beefy's done enough yet to get selected. Mind you, I don't know who else they could pick as the all-rounder. Beefy has this amazing belief in his own infallibility, it props him up. He's hardly got a run for one reason or another for a long time now, yet he'll still turn round and say he's the best all-rounder. What's more he actually thinks that as well as says it. I wouldn't have picked Neil Foster for the one-day games. We should save him for the Tests because he's going to be our number-one bowler and he does get smacked around in one-day games sometimes. We shouldn't run the risk of Fozzie losing confidence, which he sometimes does, despite his air of superiority. He's a lot more brittle mentally than he lets on. Anyway, England to win the one-day series and the Tests. A large bet if I were a big gambler. We are the better side and in a six-Test series we'll prove it.

⊖ HICK:

My birthday – 23 May. I'm twenty-three – getting old! Jackie went to take her aerobics class early in the evening, so I cooked us a meal at home and we shared a bottle of wine. That's the least I could do – I've been a little bit hard to live with this month, with a few matters on my mind. I'd come home and replay my latest failure in my mind and Jackie would say something like 'Bad luck – what happened?' We'd talk about it for a while and in the end I'd say, 'It's the wickets,' but that's too easy an option. I'd then slap a video on and forget about my batting, but at the back of my mind I know that I'm letting myself and the side down.

The following day saw the start of another championship match at New Road and another low-scoring game. Set 240 to win in sixty-one overs, Nottinghamshire finished 2 runs short with their last pair at the crease. Hick made 90 not out in the second innings off seventy-five balls, half of them from friendly bowling in search of a declaration.

⊖ HICK:

In the first innings, I was out for 9, driving a wideish one from Evans to be caught in the gully, so I was pretty keen to make amends next time. Just because they were feeding us runs didn't mean I should give my wicket away, especially as I was desperate to spend time at the crease and try to get my timing right. It was a good game of cricket but Notts should've won. Broad and Robinson gave them a good start in the second innings and, with wickets in hand, you had to fancy them. But we kept plugging away, the captain led us well and it was an encouraging effort.

DILLEY:

It was a good declaration by Phil Neale, one he wouldn't have made a few years back. It opened up the game and the spectators got their money's worth on the last day, which makes a change so far this season at New Road. With Steve Rhodes away at the one-dayers, young Stu Bevins made his first-team debut and did well. There's a rumour that the club may sign Jack Richards as cover for Steve but that won't go down very well with the players. Richards is available after being sacked by Surrey, but not only is he apparently fairly difficult to deal with, it wouldn't be fair to Stu Bevins. He's our deputy keeper on the staff and deserves a chance to see what he can do. I'll be surprised if we hear anything more about signing Jack Richards.

Good to see Eddie Hemmings having a long spell. John Emburey usually gets the nod ahead of Eddie as the England off-spinner because he keeps it tight and gets useful runs but if you're talking about entertainment value, I'd always pick Eddie. I like the way he bowls. I remember a Test in Pakistan when someone whacked him for six and four after he had tossed them both up. I was fielding at mid-on and he smiled and winked at me and tossed the next one even further up. The batter was caught. I think that's a great way to play the game. The trouble is that Eddie gets picked for a game or two, then he's out again. That does nothing for a spinner's confidence.

I had a quiet word with Chris Broad and Tim Robinson about South Africa. They've both agreed to sign and yet none of us have heard anything more since our verbal acceptance. They don't exactly see eye to eye these two: I don't imagine they'll be roommates on the tour!

Next stop, Bristol. At last the county champions put together a couple of satisfactory performances, winning the three-day game by 79 runs and the Sunday match by six wickets. Hick made 84 on the Sunday and 53 the following day in the second innings of the championship match.

⊖ HICK:

I played quite well on the Sunday and that gave me extra confidence to play even better for my 53. I enjoyed my duel with David Graveney in the second innings until I was bowled off my pads. Typical of the way I've been getting out – it was a ball where I thought, 'Forward or back?', and it rushed on a bit, hit the knee roll and went on. That was irritating because I should've got a hundred. I was out more or less the same way to Lawrence in the first innings. I have to sort out this uncertainty of when to play forward or back. I usually look to get as far forward as I can as long as I know I'm not restricting my back-foot strokes. I think that if you start to go forward when you first come in you can assess the wicket more easily and judge just how much the ball is cutting back at you or away from you. It also helps you to get away with lbws, because if you go forward and the ball pitches just outside the off-stump, the umpire ought to give you the benefit of the doubt because he has to guess whether it would have gone on to hit the stumps. After a time, once I've got the feel of the pitch, I'll be happier about playing off the back foot, as the ball gets softer and its line more predictable. The problem comes when the bounce is uneven and, although this wicket at Bristol has been a better one than any at New Road so far, I'm still uncertain about my initial movement.

It was a good contest with their bowlers. Walsh hits the seam consistently and seems to be one of those West Indians who tries as hard for his county as for his country. He doesn't get injured all that often considering all the overs he bowls. Because Lawrence lacks rhythm, one ball from him can be really quick and the next two yards slower. But he's bowling a better line this year. He's aggressive and has a big heart. Curran is a handful when he wants to be. Luckily he didn't put his back into the Sunday game after taking six wickets against us the day before. He just bowled short all the time, seemed to go through the motions and to be perfectly happy to be whacked around. It's a puzzle because he's such a good cricketer. David Graveney again impressed me with his left-arm spinners. He's the most difficult one of his type I've faced. He's really hard to get away, he varies his length well and changes his pace. He also turns it.

The most significant innings in the three-day game was played by Tim Curtis. It was a typical grafter's hundred on a pitch that tested every batter and his 102 meant we could set them more than 300 on the final day. We never thought they had a chance of that and Phil Newport swung the ball a long way to pick up more wickets. But Tim's innings won us the game. Perhaps these few days in Bristol might be the turning point in our season.

DILLEY:

I've been travelling down every day to watch the lads play and get treatment from our physio. I've been encouraged by the way we've performed these last few days – it's been much more like it. We weren't winning the Sunday game at all until right at the end when Neal Radford slogged successfully. Nine times out of ten that game would've gone their way and I reckon that's done a lot for our confidence. We won the championship match without Botham, Rhodes and myself, which underlines the strength in depth at the club. Poor Paul Bent came in to open and got a 'pair', but we cheered him up afterwards. It doesn't do to sit in the corner and brood too much. Tim Curtis played the ideal innings for the side but he got himself out in the first innings (for 23) because he was too sensitive about scoring slowly. He was grafting away when suddenly he chased a wide one and was caught behind. In the dressing room he said he'd been conscious that he wasn't scoring quickly enough and that's why he chased that one. We thought that was rubbish and told him his job is to stay out there and leave the flashing-blade stuff to the strokemakers – God knows we've got enough of them in our side. Tim is too sensitive a bloke. He should toughen up and realise how valuable he is to us playing to his own strengths.

Jack Russell got a 'pair' for them and, with the Tests coming up, we thought we might have done Steve Rhodes' chances no harm at all. Jack can bat, mind you, but I don't think he'll ever develop like Alan Knott and score Test centuries. I think he shades Steve Rhodes on basic wicket-keeping ability. He is very good, but I could never understand why people kept saying he was the best in the world when he hadn't even been picked for England. If he was *that* good, wouldn't he have got in ahead of Downton or French in the past couple of years?

Meanwhile my training is going really well and I feel terrific. We had one little scare down at Bristol when Dave Roberts listened to my knee as I was doing squat thrusts. He could hear a fair amount of clicking and he phoned the surgeon for advice. He was told it was bound to be making a noise and there was nothing to worry about. Good.

I managed to see a lot of the one-day internationals on the TV and I'm still sure we'll beat Australia when the serious stuff starts. Beefy did reasonably well, bowling tightly and smacking a few around in the last game at Lord's. Ludicrous how everybody expects him to win every game against Australia but I don't suppose he minds. Neil Foster worried me a little – he pushed a lot towards the leg-stump and he seems to be falling away at the crease. His rhythm didn't look too good and, when he bowled at the death, it wasn't going where it ought to. He's too good a bowler not to sort that out, though. I spotted an intelligent piece of bowling by Derek Pringle at Lord's. In the last over of their innings he bowled a bouncer at Tom Moody and it took him completely by surprise. He top-edged it for a couple of runs and the TV commentators tut-tutted at the idea of bowling a bouncer at that stage. But Moody was expecting each delivery to be fired into the block-hole in the usual last-over fashion and the bouncer surprised him. Why not credit the bowler for clever thinking?

On Monday, 30 May, Dilley signed a piece of paper that would mean the end of his England career later in the summer. The contract had come through from South Africa.

DILLEY:

I signed it in Bill Athey's car. He had got his solicitor to look through his contract and Bill explained a couple of points to me. His contract was the same as mine, it was a fair one and we're getting a lot of money to sign, although it means the end of our England careers. I didn't have any kind of momentous feeling, I was just exercising my rights as an individual. I know there'll be flak and I'm ready for it. If the others don't see it that way, then they're stupid. For the moment, everyone's keeping quiet. The South Africans want us to sit on it because they're still not sure if the tour is a runner and the TCCB want to pick the strongest England side this summer until at least the series is decided. Then they might start asking more direct questions than I've had to answer so far this month.

By now Harry Brind, the Test and County Cricket Board's Inspector of Pitches, was almost becoming a regular visitor to New Road, trying to help the groundsman Roy McLaren prepare more even surfaces for a fairer contest between bat and ball. Brind had been called in after the truncated match against the Australians a fortnight earlier, when the tourists had refused to play a one-day game on the free day because they were unhappy about the pitch. It seemed inevitable, in this month of Reader balls and erratic wickets, that a county would be docked twenty-five points for preparing substandard wickets.

DILLEY:

I think calling in Harry Brind makes sense. He's the TCCB's top man. It's not as if Roy McLaren is trying to rough up the pitches – we're too good a side to need an unfair advantage. I'm sure at least one county will cop the twenty-five-points deduction, but now that we've got Harry helping, it shouldn't be us. No other county has had the presence of mind to call him in early, before the deduction of points, rather than after.

The next game at New Road did nothing to still the tongues of criticism about the pitches. Glamorgan came to play a county game and a Sunday league match and again the seamers enjoyed themselves. Glamorgan were bowled out for 119 in just 27.2 overs on Sunday; while Worcestershire made 262 for 4 (Hick 50, Botham 70). The first two innings of the drawn county game totalled 261 for the loss of 20 (Hick got 43 in the first innings and did not score in the second, in which Curtis made 140 not out). Even though the championship pitch was comparatively blameless, three players were taken to hospital on Monday with injuries – one of them Ian Botham. A day after being picked to play his comeback Test against Australia, he had his cheekbone fractured in three places when he misjudged a hook shot against Steve Barwick. Early forecasts were that Botham would miss at least the next month of the season.

⊖ HICK:

The wicket was two-paced and it led to uncertainty among the batters. In the first innings, Beefy was caught off the shoulder of the bat from a forward defensive stroke and then he picked up his injury by playing too soon when Barwick bounced him. Barwick's not that quick and he had plenty of time to line up the shot, but he got too low on it and it just crept over the top of his bat. Blood started pumping out near his eye and our physio's towel was covered with it in no time. When Beefy came off he was still joking about missing an easy six runs but I think he realised it was a bad one. A few hours later, we were asked by the captain to go into the dressing room, told what had happened to Beefy and instructed to say nothing to pressmen who were gathered in the bar. It's rough on Beefy, but he's got back from worse than this one and he'll do it again. Trouble is that everyone will start going on even more about the wickets at home, especially as Phil Neale and their wicket-keeper Colin Metson were also taken to hospital for stitches on the same day. But Phil's was a fluke. The ball got up, he tried to get out of the way and it hit him on the chin strap of his helmet. He was lucky he was wearing a helmet. Metson misjudged the flight of the ball as it came through to him behind the stumps. It went through his gloves and smacked him on the face. You can't blame that one on the pitch. But the doubts are still there for those of us who spend a lot of time at New Road, and a day like Monday just puts more pressure on the groundsman, worries our batters even more and annoys our supporters, who'd like to see proper cricket.

As for the two games, I played reasonably well on the Sunday until I went to turn one to leg. It bounced and, when I tried to pull out of the shot, I got a leading edge and it just looped up. We just bowled better than them on the Sunday, with Beefy and Newport swinging the ball skilfully. In the county match, I was disappointed to be adjudged lbw in the first innings after I pushed forward to a slower one and it hit me a long way down the track. I was just beginning to feel back in some sort of nick then. Second innings, a nought – and a pretty standard one, second ball caught at slip. On the final day, rain ended any hopes of a decent finish but Tim Curtis deserves a mention: no one else got over 40 in the championship match but he got 140 not out against decent bowlers trying to get us out. TC is a great man in a crisis, and that's what we are in with batters dropping like flies.

⊂▬ DILLEY:

It wasn't the wicket itself that did for Beefy: he was early on the shot. But this wicket now has such a reputation that the papers will call it a 'terror track' because three players had stitches. But Colin Metson was done by the ball coming on at him, rather than dying in the flight, while Phil Neale top-edged a hook. I wouldn't have thought that hooking on this uneven pitch was a good idea, but then I'm not a batter. The basic problem is that no one knows what the ball's going to do when it pitches and sooner or later one will get you out. So the batters are jumpy and tend to blame all their defects on the pitch. I can understand that. We are playing this game for a living and we want to give of our best. But our batters aren't getting stuck in like they did last year, when we thought we'd win the game if we got 250 because we were good enough to bowl most sides out twice on helpful wickets. Perhaps we should look a little harder at ourselves, instead of looking for scapegoats.

Of course we're all sorry for Beefy, especially after working so hard to get back into the game – but remember we won the title without him last year and we can cope without him again. Having played cricket with him for so long, I never really expect to see him hurt, but there was a fair amount of blood pumping into Dave Roberts' towel. To be honest I didn't think he was ready for Test cricket again. He's bowling sensibly on helpful pitches but at number six he needs runs behind him and he's short of them so far. He'll be back – he needs the game too much to drift away, feeling sorry for himself.

The fitness training is going well for me – up to three times a day and I feel great. I've done hardly any bowling yet but I hope that turns out to be something I haven't forgotten how to do – the same applies to one or two other things. I almost played on the Sunday, but we left it for another week. To my surprise Micky Stewart rang the club to check on my fitness before they picked the squad for the First Test. I think it's ridiculous that they should even consider me. Fast bowling needs hard work and match practice before you can even approach something like a Test match with confidence. I never had a chance for Leeds and it would've been totally unfair if someone who'd bowled consistently well throughout May was pushed out because Graham Dilley thought he could get through a five-day Test without match practice. Sometimes I do think it's harder to get out of the England squad than to get into it when I hear things like that.

I'm pleased that Phil Newport is in the squad because he's put in the performances and deserves a shot at someone other than Sri Lanka. I agree with DeFreitas and Pringle – Daffy looks sharp and keen and gets bounce, while Pring's a better bowler than David Capel. They've picked John Emburey as the sole spinner but I would've also picked a left-arm spinner for balance. The batting picks itself, it looks strong and should look after itself against what I think is a rather plain Australian bowling line-up. The game's at Leeds, which is worrying the Aussies because of recent history, and I reckon we can go one-up right away.

As May slipped into June, Graeme Hick was still searching for runs – but first he needed the confidence in matches that would enable him to churn them out in the manner expected of him. Talk of a thousand runs in May had long been dropped and Hick chose an unusual setting to try to bat his way back into form.

HICK:

We played two days in a row for Paul Pridgeon in benefit matches and I was annoyed at getting out in the first one, caught one-handed for nought. The players took the mickey out of me and they had an even bigger laugh later on when a chap came up to me and asked me something I just couldn't understand. The game was at Lye – in the Black Country between Kidderminster and Birmingham, where they speak a particular accent that baffles someone brought up in Southern Africa. I first thought this chap had said to me that his mother had died. I said, 'I'm sorry to hear that,' but he still kept on at me. I called over Paul Pridgeon, who comes from round those parts, and he translated for me. Apparently the question was 'What's more difficult, keeping wicket or facing Malcolm Marshall?'

Next day, we went to another benefit match, at Elmley Castle, a nice little village not far from Worcester. It may have just been on the village green but by now I'm desperate to get runs, so I set myself to bat a long time and have a net out in the middle. Apparently I looked very keen when I scampered a sharp single to get off nought. The very least I wanted was fifty but I kept going, hit a few sixes and Pridge told me it was okay to stay in till the end of the innings. Near the end Steve Rhodes came out to join me and I could tell he was annoyed that I'd stayed in so long. When we fielded he gave me some fearful stick, calling me 'Boycs' and 'Geoff', but I took no notice and just smiled. It felt good to get some runs again and a hundred's a hundred – even at Elmley Castle.

I'm a little down that I haven't got very near to another thousand runs in May. In the winter I'd thought about the fact that nobody had ever got it two seasons in a row, so I looked at the fixture list and hoped for a good start. The big hundred against the MCC was a bonus, but since then I've struggled. I wouldn't say this openly but I see no reason why I can't get a thousand runs in May again if I play properly and have some luck with wickets and weather. You have to aim high in this game. But this time I've felt that even if I was in better form I would've struggled to get many runs. The mood is negative, and the footwork isn't positive enough. After a while people are coming up to me and saying things like 'Not the usual Graeme Hick today,' and I'll smile and say, 'Well, it just shows you I'm human.' They're well-meaning fans of the club so it's important to keep a sense of humour, but I'm looking forward to a few comments like 'Well played, Graeme' as soon as possible.

COMEBACKS AND SETBACKS

For the first time in a month, Dilley rejoined Hick and his colleagues for first-team action. With Ian Botham injured and Phil Newport away on Test duty, Dilley's return was timely. Figures of 5 for 42 in Derbyshire's first innings pleased him almost as much as another championship win, this time by 145 runs.

DILLEY:

I got a wicket with my first spell on the first evening and, as I walked off at close of play, this press guy said to me, 'Will you be ringing Ted Dexter?' What a stupid question! I mumbled something like, 'If he wants me he knows where I am,' but I knew perfectly well that that bloke wanted a headline to scream 'Dilley Roars Out Warning to Lord Ted.' Pathetic. It's too early to judge the progress, even though the scorecard says I did well. You have to feel happy that every ball you're delivering is going somewhere near where you want it to. If you want to play in a Test match you've got to approach that standard, otherwise you get smashed around the park. Last year, just before we played the West Indies at Lord's, my line and rhythm were so perfect when we played Hampshire that I could eventually do away with fine leg because nothing was going down there. I'm nowhere near that yet, but it's starting to come back. Maybe 5 for 42 flattered me but I did get four of the top six and that is part of my job.

We beat Derbyshire because we batted better in the second innings and set them a stiff target on yet another interesting pitch. Paul Bent, one of our young hopefuls, came in and played well for 62. Phil Neale reckons he times the ball better than anyone else on the staff and he did look a fair player. You can't expect someone to come from the seconds and cream it all over the place but Benty handled the transition well in this game. When they batted again, they were soon 0 for 2 thanks to Neal Radford and there's not much chance in that situation of getting nearly 300. You look to put pressure on the opposition batters right from the start and this is one area where I think we do very well. We expect wickets. Radford is an ideal man for these kinds of pitches. He gets a lot of people lbw because he bowls so straight. He's also quicker than he looks. Radders is looking very confident because he's getting wickets (six in the second innings) and runs at the moment – he's a very handy slogger, particularly on Sundays – not that confidence is ever a problem with Radders. We know how to take him down a peg or two, though – steal his comb for a start. Then tell him certain other seamers that he doesn't rate look like England bowlers.

Phil Neale thoughtfully eased me through the Sunday game, which we won comfortably. He knows I don't like the Sunday stuff. This may be coloured by the fact that in the past the shortened run-up hasn't helped my rhythm. If you need a thirty-yard run-up to make you feel right when you arrive at the wicket, there's no point in trying to run off twenty-two. There are times at the death when I enjoy the challenge of the Sunday game, but basically I think it's entertainment rather than cricket. It's a great fund-raiser and it gets people through the turnstiles, but in terms of bringing on young players it's a complete waste of time. The last thing you want to do is play on the Sunday, get involved in all the strain of a tight finish, then have to go out and field on the Monday morning in a championship match. You're still mentally tired because you've been concentrating so hard. The genuine cricket-lovers I talk to don't really enjoy the Sunday stuff either. The sneerers, the out-of-season soccer yobs who love taking the piss out of big lumps like me and Derek Pringle see it differently. The admission fee gives them a licence to get pissed and make a noise. I like humorous barracking – in Australia once one guy shouted out, 'Hey, Willis! You take ugly pills – in fact I reckon you're hooked on them' – but over here it's all pretty moronic. It's all part and parcel of modern sport. Any respect that the public might have had for the performers has disappeared because the media have made sportsmen so familiar. You don't know someone from Adam, yet he feels he can come up to you and say what he likes. Too many of that type turn up on Sundays.

Anyway, enough of my moaning. We've beaten Derbyshire twice over one weekend and we're beginning to look like a decent side again. The results have to come our way, otherwise there's no point in this profession. I keep telling the boys that Kent were bottom of the table by mid-June in 1970, yet they went on to win it. We can do the same. It's not just a football cliché about taking each game as it comes.

⊖ HICK:

Dill bowled very well on a wicket that didn't really suit him. He's back at the right time, because Paul Pridgeon has torn an Achilles and he would've been very useful, filling in for Newport and Botham. Pridge bowls straight and he's particularly handy in the one-day games. At his age, you don't come back all that quickly from an Achilles tear.

Dill didn't slip himself in this match – he was just concentrating on line and length. That's more or less what he's done since he came to Worcester and that makes sense because he would've been sidelined with even more knee trouble if he'd roared in day after day. He's very hard to play when he gets it right – moving the ball a little through the air, getting it to go off the seam when it pitches. He's the best strike bowler England have got. He was pleased but he didn't say much. He just gets on with the job, tries his best on the field and hopes it comes off. He won't get carried away with success at this stage of his career.

I got myself out in both innings of the championship match. In the first, I played at a wide one on 17, rooted to the crease rather than making a positive move back or forward. It left me slightly and I was caught at third slip. I'd been driving the ball quite well, with the left foot getting to the pitch of the ball, but I wasn't going all that much for the cut. The variation in bounce made me worried that I'd drag it on, so I was waiting for the really wide ones. Instinctively I was still guessing where the ball would go and I felt restricted in my strokeplay. In the second innings, I was caught behind on 42 by Bernie Maher off a ball that bounced and got high on the bat. It wasn't a great stroke but I felt I had time to watch the ball on to the bat. Footwork again. Just before, Bernie Maher had said, 'You're looking good,' and that had pleased me. I was trying to play the ball a little later than usual because of the erratic bounce, but this time I got it wrong and the extra bounce did me. On Sunday I was caught behind trying to run it down to third man and I got a faint edge. I play that shot quite happily in the one-day games because often there isn't a slip or a third man and there's a chance of three runs because the nearest fielder has to run from cover. A productive shot, but it can get you out if your timing isn't right.

Martin Weston helped win us the Sunday game on 11 June with 72 and a couple of wickets. I think he's a very underrated cricketer and with Beefy set to be missing for a time he can build on the good season he had last year when he took the all-rounder's position. People have said in the past that his days are numbered at Worcester but I've always rated him. I played a lot with him in the seconds – we once put on over 400 – and he whacks the ball with a simple, effective technique. He also gets bounce when he bowls his medium-pacers. Successful sides all have a Martin Weston. He likes a bet, does Wesso, and sometimes he forgets about a horse he'd told us about three weeks ago. He doesn't forget for himself, though. He's just landed a winner at twenty to one and we gave him heaps for forgetting to remind us. Wesso, Paul Pridgeon and Steve O'Shaughnessy follow the form very closely and then give us the benefit of their judgements. Beefy has a little dabble now and then. Correction – a large dabble. We only hear from him about the ones that finished first.

My parents have just arrived. They come over every summer for at least a month and they were full of the impending grandchild. I must say I'm beginning to feel the same way. Mum and Dad came to the Derbyshire game and Mum noticed straightaway that I was batting differently. She said I was crouching too much, instead of using my height and getting over the ball. She's probably right – mothers notice these things about their sons and she does know a fair amount about the game. It would explain the anxiety in my batting I've felt all summer so far. I'll try to get some runs for them while they're here. Dad will tell you he was the finest slow left-arm spinner ever seen in the local leagues back home, but he was a handy bowler, and he's scored a hundred in the league as well. His best sport was tennis. For a time he was the best young player in Rhodesia and would've come over to play Junior Wimbledon but he decided to throw in his lot with farming. He and I used to partner each other in doubles when I was still at school – of course we were invincible!

While Worcestershire gradually inched their way towards some form, England had a nightmare game at Leeds, losing on the final afternoon as their second innings disintegrated against accurate seam bowling by Terry Alderman. David Gower was already being panned in some newspapers for his decision to put Australia in after winning the toss, and three days later England could only look to salvage a draw as the Australians declared on 601 for 7. They failed, surprisingly.

DILLEY:

I don't think any other captain would've batted on that first morning. Gower was right to put them in, on the grounds of the recent history of Leeds Tests, the fact that the Aussies were worried stiff about Headingley and the fact that the muggy conditions were absolutely right for the bowlers. You can't blame David for the fact that his bowlers didn't do a proper job. Mark Taylor's knock on the first day was important to them. Tim Curtis kept saying, 'He'll get out soon,' because he fancied Phil Newport to do him with swing bowling. Taylor looks fairly flat-footed and when he was driving his foot wasn't really moving out to the pitch of the ball, away from the stumps, so he had to be candidate for the lbw from a nip-backer or an inswinger. But it didn't swing for some reason.

I thought Allan Lamb's hundred was terrific entertainment. He relies on his eye and, if it swings or seams around, he can struggle, but he has a terrific temperament and loves to fight it out. A great guy to play cricket with, Lamby. Once when I was playing for Kent on a slow pitch at Canterbury, he came in, got a single off the first ball and said to me, 'Picca, I don't think I need a helmet on this wicket.' So next time I bowled at him, I bounced one, it hit him on the back of the head and it bounced over the keeper for four leg-byes. We had a good laugh about that. Lamby's part of a very powerful middle order England can put out – Gatting, Gower, Smith, Botham – so as long as Gooch and Broad lay the foundations, I can see us getting stacks of runs against the Aussies. I still think we'll beat them this summer. Headingley must be seen as a one-off. They'd been looking to get away with a draw all the game and Border even delayed his declaration on the final morning. Then we lost a couple of wickets and they scented victory. Never underestimate the importance of pressure in Test cricket. As soon as a side has 600 runs on the board, the other one will struggle. I don't think they'll play as well again and we won't bowl as badly again.

HICK:

We arrived in Leeds by a coincidence on that final evening, not long after England had lost. We were on our way up to Harrogate to play in the Tilcon Trophy and we took a detour to have fish and chips at Bryan's. The restaurant is just beside the cricket ground and it's a favourite spot for players and cricket fans. So we walk in, go to our table and these four guys followed us in. They were obviously the worse for wear and hadn't enjoyed the beating handed out to England. They went through the entire Test while waiting to order. 'What a terrible shot by Gower,' 'Why field on the first day on a flat wicket?', 'Why didn't they play a spinner?' It was basically all the stuff they would've heard on the TV or the radio and we couldn't stop listening to them because they were so loud. Finally one of them said, 'What are we going to do then?' and another replied, 'Let's get this Hick bloke qualified and have him in by the end of the series.' We all burst out laughing, but they still didn't recognise us, they were so engrossed in their conversation. Phil Neale asked if he should introduce me to them, but I don't think it was the right moment for a chat!

Worcester then played two games in Harrogate for the Tilcon Trophy. The teams knocked out in the qualifying stages of the Benson and Hedges Cup are considered, provided there are gaps in the fixture list, and this year, Sussex, Surrey and Yorkshire joined Worcestershire. The trophy (and £1500) was won this time by Worcestershire, who beat Surrey in the final by five wickets. Hick (80 and 43) enjoyed the trip.

HICK:

The last time we played in the Tilcon it rained for three days and we ended up bowling at a stump on matting to find a winner. This time the weather was fine, a good crowd turned up on every day and there was a nice atmosphere. They weren't pressure games – no one was running in trying to knock your head off – but it wasn't hit-and-giggle stuff like a benefit match. In the first game against Sussex I hit a couple over mid-off early on and suddenly felt good. I hit a couple of straight sixes later. Next day I got a quick 40-odd and then got out trying to hit one over the top. But I walked back with a smile on my face because I got out to a shot that I hadn't dared to play so far this season. Maybe the touch and the timing are on their way back. Perhaps Mum put her finger on it: I know I'm standing up taller now at the crease.

On the day we weren't playing, we went to Beefy's house near Darlington for a barbecue and he treated us brilliantly. He's got twenty-six acres of land, a trout stream and so many gadgets to keep us all amused. Dave Roberts and I caught some trout – I do a lot of fishing back in Zimbabwe and it was nice to have a net! Some of the others had time trials on a four-wheel motorbike in a field round the back while I fished. The guys were tearing around and a few of them came off at speed. We did some clay-pigeon shooting too. It was a terrific day because we felt glad to get away from the public responsibilities for a while and just relax as a group. Beefy is a great host, he's so generous and he also delegates well. Andy, his personal assistant, seems to do most of the chores while Beefy is lord of all he surveys and enters into all the fun. At some parties you see the host running around all over the place, worrying that everyone is sorted out with drinks and food, but Beefy gets it right. I don't know whether we treat him differently from when he was at Somerset, but I know how happy he is with us. Perhaps that's because we won't believe in any of that superstar stuff and he gets his leg pulled as much as the rest. Maybe he's found a lot of honest friendships among the Worcestershire players: we take him just the way he is.

We always have a laugh when Beefy and Tim Curtis start arguing. Now Tim is a clever guy while Beefy is streetwise, but no academic. Tim always loses me in an argument. I enjoy arguing just for the sake of it though, and yet he does me easily. I then resort to calling him a gin-and-tonic cricketer because he's so clever (nothing could be further from the truth – I admire his professionalism but that's another story). But Beefy tries to bash his way through Tim's argument by force, yet as soon as Tim starts using words of five or six syllables, Beefy starts to bite and you know he's done. It's terrific value and the entertainment it gives the rest of us just shows what a happy side we are.

Worcestershire returned to serious competition at the weekend with a comfortable win by 22 runs over Warwickshire at Edgbaston. The Refuge champions of 1988 were beginning to find their touch. Dilley had several reasons for satisfaction that weekend – for a change, he bowled well in the Sunday game (3 for 30 off his eight overs), and he was picked for the Second Test at Lord's in a few days' time.

━━▶ DILLEY:

Between the Derbyshire game that finished on 13 June and the Test which starts on the 22nd I shall have bowled eight overs in first-team cricket. That shows the stupidity of our system – one moment we're being bowled into the ground, the next we don't have any games for a fortnight. It's all so lop-sided. I've worked very hard to get fit and there's a strong feeling of personal satisfaction in achieving something that doesn't come naturally, but I'm worried about my match fitness. I have to take into consideration that I could be in the field at Lord's for two days, especially as the wicket will probably be a flat one.

Anyway I actually got some wickets at last in the Sunday slog today, my first of the season and probably my last. I got Reeve, Humpage and Lloyd, not the worst trio. I also bowled Paul Smith with a no-ball. It was quite funny actually – it dipped into him and he went arse over tit, hit him on the foot and then the stumps. We did well to beat them because 194 isn't a large total to defend in forty overs. Instead of trying to push it around they tried to hit boundaries and we exerted enough pressure on them to induce mistakes. Pretty standard stuff for a Sunday – all very boring, apart from the need to maintain our run.

HICK:

I was in a long time for 35 not out. It was hard to get going on a slow pitch and I didn't get much of the strike early in my knock. I was very lucky against Alan Donald. He beat me with a yorker, the ball hit the base of the leg-stump, the bail jumped up, popped back into the groove, and the ball went for four byes. At his pace, the bail should've fallen off but I'm not complaining. At first the runs were credited to me but I made the mistake of looking at the stumps and they changed it to byes. Donald is quick and he's getting a bit of a reputation for putting players in hospital. He looks a good athlete and he seems to be getting faster every season. I think we'll have to wait and see him on quick wicket before we can judge just how sharp he is. He's a little chest-on but he gets the ball to move away from the bat. At the moment I'd have to say that Graham Dilley is quicker.

We forced this win because they got bogged down against the demon spin of yours truly and Richard Illingworth and then they needed boundaries in a hurry. We gambled by keeping a lot of fielders inside the circle to enourage them to try hitting over the top and it worked. I managed a run-out when Dermot Reeve called Asif Din for a sharp single – Hick pounced à la Roger Harper and lobbed it into the keeper and Asif was stranded.

With Worcestershire again idle for a couple of days, Paul Pridgeon managed to fit in a couple of functions for his benefit. To his dismay, Hick found himself the innocent victim of a misunderstanding.

HICK:

We're due to play a cricket match for Pridge at Barnt Green, which is about twelve miles from Birmingham. Unfortunately the local papers are full of Beefy making his comeback there after his injury and my presence is also advertised. I don't know why Beefy isn't playing, but I do know that I told Pridge and the organisers some time ago that I couldn't make it. My parents have to go home early because my sister needs them there, with her first baby due, and I wanted to spend one of their last full days here with them. So what will the locals think when they see I haven't turned up? I always honour my commitments and try to get there on time and be pleasant to people, and I don't like anyone thinking I've let them down. So I turned up for a drink in the bar after the match just to make sure they understood. We're on our way up to Sheffield for a county game, so it all tied in.

DILLEY:

I had a good day at Stourbridge Golf Club, playing for Pridge. These days are always well organised and invariably you're part-nered by nice people. I remember once though when one bloke took it far too seriously. I was supposed to be their best player, as I was then playing off a fifteen handicap, but I never cracked on that I was all that good. Anyway, we're on the seventeenth with no chance of winning and I'm lining up a forty-foot putt when this guy comes over to me and says, 'Now come on, if you get this in we could win the competition.' Not much pressure on me there – if I'd holed that one, I'd be giving interviews to Peter Alliss and playing golf for a living. I enjoy the game, but my best asset is that I can find the ball. I'm a deadly spotter, much in demand among my team-mates who look to hit the ball miles. I try to be a canny player but when I do attempt to play seriously and hit off the tee with an iron, rather than a wood, I whack it out of bounds or into a bunker. Most of our lads are good players, approaching single-figure handicaps. Mine is anything between twelve and sixteen. Young Hick simply murders the ball – he takes a big wind-up and it disappears. I'm a right-handed player, even though

I bat left. That's because I couldn't get any left-handed clubs when I started playing.

I left Stourbridge to go down to London two days early for the Test match. The rail strike means motorways are a nightmare at the moment and I wanted some hard work in the nets at Lord's, so I could be more confident about facing the Aussies than I felt when I was selected. We've just had our team dinner the night before the start and the mood was reasonably jovial. We know that the Headingly result has made things harder for us, but we have to perform with more discipline in batting and bowling. Marsh and Taylor run a lot of quick singles, so watch out for them – and Jones is the same. Don't give Taylor too much width or half-volleys because he likes to drive, and try to frustrate Marsh because he's a limited player. Don't forget that Border hits it in the air when he picks one up off his legs. Don't give any width to Jones and Waugh. You come away from the team dinner thinking you know how to get all of them out, but we all know that it's totally different out there on the field than the night before, sipping Château E. R. Dexter. David Gower was his usual relaxed self at the dinner. His whole aura is totally in contrast to Mike Gatting's. David doesn't build up a Test into the ultimate cricketing test, he thinks you perform and concentrate well when you're relaxed. Gatt was much more intense, less articulate. It all depends on the individual, but I favour the Gower approach. After the usual juvenile humour around the table, we break up. I hope we bat first tomorrow, I prefer to get into the match before I'm called on to do my stuff. I feel more pressure on me when I'm running in to bowl the first ball of the Test match.

Day One: England 286 (Russell 64, Gooch 60, Gower 57). Australia 1/0.

DILLEY:

A poor total on a good wicket. Gooch's dismissal was the key one. He was out just after lunch when we needed him to anchor things as the others played a lot of shots. I thought we were scoring too quickly, but you can't tell our batsmen to block the next delivery after they've hit the last three for four. We did play a little rashly at times, though. Jack Russell played very well. He'd worked out his own way to combat Merv Hughes' aggression. I hung around with him to add a few for the last wicket and I was rather flatterd when Merv 'sledged' me. I played a ball of full length away through the covers and he snarled, 'That's the last one you get in your half, Picca.' He rather spoiled the effect by calling me by my nickname, though! I was bloody annoyed when I got out, nibbling at Alderman to be caught at slip. I'd told myself just to play straight, not to touch the stuff outside the off-stump. Incidentally, Terry Alderman's responsible for a phrase Micky Stewart has used ever since he came on to the scene as England manager. When we played together at Kent, Terry was asked where he bowled. He said, 'Jeez mate, I just bowl in the corridor of uncertainty – on or around off-stump.' He does too. So Micky's 'corridor of uncertainty' comes via me from an original idea of Terry Alderman's. I'm afraid he's putting too many in that corridor at the moment.

We had one over at them tonight and the omens aren't good. Marsh played me away square on the off-side for a single and when the ball came back to me, a big chunk of leather was missing on the shiny side. That's going to be fun bowling on a flat wicket with the ball knackered. We'll see if we can persuade the umpires to change it tomorrow.

Day Two: Australia 269/6 (Boon 94, Waugh 35 not out).

DILLEY:

We had a reasonable final session when we took a few bonus wickets and we're still in the game. I thought Foster bowled brilliantly and Jarvis quickly in the last hour. For a little bloke Jarvo generates a lot of pace – he has a fast arm action and good rhythm. I didn't bowl very well. I just couldn't get going. I had early encouragement when I got Marsh with an outswinger, but it never really fell into place. The bloody ball was shot to pieces after twelve overs and the umpires wouldn't change it because it hadn't gone out of shape or been deliberately damaged. It was soft, the seam was almost non-existent and a few chunks were missing. Thank you very much. So we bowled with that piece of soap for eighty-four overs before we got a new one. When I got David Boon caught at slip off a ball that swung, that just proved to me that they'd have been in trouble if we'd been given the chance to swing it with a decent ball. Once the ball is up to them, these Aussies seem to hit through the line of it. I'm even more convinced we can bowl them out this summer.

Day Three: Australia 528 (Waugh 152 not out, Lawson 74), England 58/3.

DILLEY:

Black Saturday. A shocker. I bowled like a drain. Paul Jarvis and I went for around four an over all day and I can't imagine how bad it would've been without the steadiness of Neil Foster and John Emburey. I suppose we have to console ourselves that everybody at some stage in their Test career will bat well, but why did Geoff Lawson choose today? We know that Lawson doesn't fancy the short stuff and we did bounce him, but on this flat wicket it only got up waist high and even he can play those. We didn't bowl particularly well at Waugh – he got exactly the same sort of offerings as he did at Leeds. He smacked it when it was short and outside the off-stump. We just didn't get the ball in the right place. It's not a nice feeling going in to bat on the Saturday night, knowing you've got to bat bloody well to save the game. That needs as much concentration as Thursday morning, at the start. We blew it in the first hour of our innings, losing three good wickets. Gooch went in the first over and he's the man we were looking to for a long innings of 150 plus. Broad got a faint in-side ledge and it knocked out his off-pole. How many times did Waugh get away with that at Leeds and here? We've lost bloody count. David Gower blocked it out well at the end and he seemed his usual self afterwards when he was rushing to get to the press conference and then on to the theatre with some of the lads. Word came back that he'd walked out of the press conference and automatically we sided with him. The old 'them and us' syndrome. The papers should make interesting reading tomorrow.

Sunday, 25 June – rest day in the Lord's Test.

DILLEY:

The papers have had a field day. David's walkout gave them the story they wanted and we've copped it good and hard. Trying very hard to be fair, I can understand how it must be difficult to report a day like yesterday and not get caught up in the atmosphere of dismay at England's performance. I'm sure some of them are praying for more bad news because that sells papers. Most of them were well wide of the mark in their assessments. Nothing about the knackered ball, the luck that Waugh had with inside edges or Broady's bad luck with his dismissal. Hardly any praise for Foster and Emburey and far too much drivel about Gower getting us bowling at the wrong ends. Fozzie was quite happy bowling from the Pavilion End and he told the captain so, and quite rightly he left him there – but the press keep nagging at this one, saying that he never bowls well from that end at Lord's. Well, he did yesterday. A captain asks his bowlers where they fancy bowling and does his best to accommodate them. Where could David turn to when two of his four front-line bowlers were getting hammered? You can't blame the captain for our inadequacies – he doesn't bowl the ball.

This stuff about the captain attending the Saturday night press conference is a load of nonsense. Why should David go there when he's had to bat for an hour after a very bad day and justify himself? Why do these guys who sit up in the press box all day need quotes? They should give their own opinions and not need David Gower's version of the day's play. I would always support the right of the cricket writers to climb into any of us on matters of cricket – but don't expect us to do their job for them when we know we've cocked it up and that they're going to slam us in print.

I'm very anti-press conferences anyway after last year's fiasco at Lord's. I took a few wickets against the West Indies and I was asked to talk to the media. I hadn't forgotten the way the press had pissed on me in New Zealand and I wasn't keen. But I was told I'd be in breach of contract and that Tony Lewis would be doing it for BBC TV so it would be handled in the proper manner. The first thing he said in the interview was: 'Well done – and you did it without a sign of temper.' That did it for me. I then had to attend a press conference because I'd done the TV interview and I was in no mood to be stuffed again. I then decided I would not co-operate in the future when I was playing for England and I told Micky Stewart that. I'll just have to pay the fine when I refuse. Any more performances like this one and nobody will want to interview me anyway!

Day Four – England 322/9, a lead of 80 (Gower 106, Smith 96, Alderman 6/128).

DILLEY:

We're almost down the pan, but today we made them fight. Gower was always a banker for a hundred after the hammering from the media – he has a lot of character and a great temperament. Just because he takes things gently doesn't mean he's less gritty than anyone else when he buckles on his pads. He and Robin Smith played superbly. The one that got Robin was an absolute beauty. Alderman bowled one that pitched middle and leg and hit the top of the off. You can only hope to get a little nick on ones like that. Robin had been batting four hours and even then it was unplayable. At the end, I hung around a few overs with John Emburey, playing quite well, doing nothing stupid and hoping it pours down tomorrow. Bet it doesn't.

Day Five – England 359, AUSTRALIA 119/4. Australia won by six wickets.

━━▶ DILLEY:

We might have got away with this with a bit of luck. Embers and I added 45 for the last wicket and the rain threatened. They got more and more frustrated and I was very annoyed when I got an inside edge to be caught by Boon at short leg. My mind kept going back to the Old Trafford Test last year when the West Indies rolled us over ten minutes before a thunderstorm flooded the ground on the final day. I kept trying to hang on with Embers, but then I got my feet in a tangle, ended up playing across my front pad and got a nick. Obviously we were set for a beating, but we went out there and tried everything. I got a lucky wicket early on when Marsh played no stroke – it seamed back a long way and took his off-stump. I got everything wrong, just let it go, and he was unlucky enough to get about the only ball from me that did much in the game. Then Taylor was caught in the slips just before lunch. It then poured down but unfortunately only during the lunch interval, so that the actual delay was about three-quarters of an hour. Fozzie got Border and Jones cheaply and they were a little twitchy at 76 for 4. Border's dismissal was a pleasing one. We'd said before that he tends to flick the ball in the air to leg – David Capel got him out that way in the Bicentenary Test at Sydney last year – and he fell for it again here. It was a great moment for young Robin Sims, who was subbing for Robin Smith. He's a lad on the MCC groundstaff and the day meant so much for him. Any catch is a good catch when you come on as sub in a Test, but when the ball's in the air for a long time from the bat of the Australian captain and there's a glimmer of hope for us if he can catch it – that becomes the catch of a genuine cricketer. You should've seen the colour of him when we ran across to congratulate him. He was shaking and all the colour had gone from his face. It was a lovely moment.

In the end they got home easily enough. The rain didn't save us and we didn't deserve to be saved, I suppose. In the dressing room afterwards we just didn't believe we had lost twice in a row to them. Waugh will be all the rage for a time now, but we haven't bowled well at him or the others. We just didn't bowl a consistent line and make them work hard for their runs. I just hope I can start to bowl better. I need some overs under my belt. I'm worried about no-balls and I'm not getting to the wicket at the right speed – I'm falling away and just putting it there. To get over this, I just have to bowl and bowl, and get some rhythm.

So it's off to our hotel in Peterborough to play Cambridgeshire in the NatWest Cup. Just our luck if we get rolled over by another fluke. On with the tapes in the car and try to forget about cricket for a few hours. Thank God Micky Stewart didn't ask me anything more about South Africa. Now that I've signed it would be rather difficult answering a straight question. Perhaps Micky's got too much on his mind to bother about South Africa.

While Dilley was struggling at Lord's, Worcestershire played two more championship games and a Sunday league match. They failed to win any of them. The first – at Sheffield against Yorkshire – was drawn after Worcestershire took a big first-innings lead of 140 and tried to bowl them out a second time; but Yorkshire scored 280 for 4. For Hick, there was some personal consolation, an innings of 150 off 156 balls.

⊏══➤ HICK:

It was one of the best wickets we've come across so far this season. Mum and Dad were there to see my innings, so I'm pleased they saw something of my usual form before they flew back. I got myself out just after tea when I could've been there for another hour and got a double hundred. The captain had told me he wanted to crack on for a declaration and in the first over after tea I hit three good boundaries, then got caught behind trying to run a wide one down to third man. That running-down shot again! I'm more angry about getting in such a situation than when I go cheaply, because I'm seeing the ball big and well past the hundred.

They batted a long time in the game without getting many runs and I think that's all credit to our bowlers. We felt we'd bowl them out in the second innings but the wicket seemed to stay just the same as on the first two days. Beefy bowled well in his first game back after his fractured cheekbone. There wasn't a lot of pace in the wicket and he beat the bat a lot. He bowled forty-nine overs in the match for his three wickets and I think he wanted to prove he should've been picked for the Lord's Test because he was fit enough. But the cheekbone injury is still troubling him even though he doesn't admit it, and he's still short of form and runs with the bat. He'll probably prove me wrong in the next game against Middlesex.

He didn't. Botham had another disappointing four days from 24 to 27 June – scores of 47, 6 and 8, and just five wickets in three innings, as Middlesex did the double over Worcestershire in both championship (by nine wickets) and Refuge Assurance (by five wickets). Seventeen wickets fell on the first day of the championship game as the wicket again suffered from uneven bounce.

HICK:

I got 5 and 6 in the championship game, and 5 on Sunday. Angus Fraser bowled me twice – chopping one on in the first innings, then he hit the base of my middle stump as the ball just crept over my toe when I expected one around waist height. I wanted a good score against Middlesex because they're such a good bowling side, but at the moment it doesn't matter which of our lads walks out at New Road with a bat in his hand, because he doesn't expect to survive very long. It's all a subconscious thing for us now – the opposition players who come here don't take any notice, so they do better. They don't have that sinking feeling we've had after just a few overs of almost every game here this season. Botham and Weston approached the problem in their usual positive manner by smashing a few boundaries before they were picked off. We are all getting thoroughly cheesed off and the batters are chipping at the bowlers in the dressing room. We go out to bat and get hardly anything loose to score off, yet Neal Radford, for example, keeps bowling too full a length and they can hit him for a few fours. We never seem to get those gifts at the moment. We'll stand in the slips and call it the RSM – the Radford School of Motoring, for learning to drive. Up till now, Radders has bowled really well, but he's going through a bad patch just when we need him at his tightest.

Middlesex are like Essex – very hard to beat with their good bowlers and positive approach. Their senior players set high standards and when they lose guys to the Tests they seem to be able to withstand that. We were very disappointed with our two performances against them in one weekend. They did us by five wickets on the Sunday, when we were bowled out for only 143. That's simply not good enough, nor was my shot that got me out – trying to pull one that kept a little low and took the off-stump. Wrong stroke selection. I don't play the pull shot all that often – I tend to nurdle it around to leg if necessary. I prefer leaving the short stuff and concentrate on playing straight.

We lost the championship game inside two days and Phil Neale had a word about that one and Sunday's game in the dressing room. He stressed we were all in the same boat and had to hang together. We had to stop thinking, 'What the hell's the ball going to do now?' We knew that visiting batters were wondering what all the fuss was about and that a lot of it was in the mind. He told us that it was vital to keep the team spirit going with July just around the corner and hopes fading of another championship/Sunday league double. We knew he was right, but it all needed saying. Tomorrow we're on for a giant-killing act at the hands of Cambridgeshire, so we'll have to be at our most professional. An early exit from the NatWest Cup at the hands of a Minor Counties team isn't a nice thought.

It didn't happen, and Hick had much to do with that. He made 86 not out, Tim Curtis scored an unbeaten 91 and Worcestershire cruised home at 206 for 1 with nearly twelve overs to spare, after restricting Cambridgeshire to 202 for 4. The match was over on the first allotted day, always a pleasant sequel for the worried county cricketer who dreads such games and also looks forward to a couple of days off.

◯ HICK:

They were a reasonable side, with nothing to lose, and I thought it was a satisfactory performance by us. The ground in the small town of March was lovely, with poplar trees running along one side, the hospitality was friendly and the tea-ladies couldn't do enough for us. They'd put up a few marquees, the atmosphere was very friendly and I can honestly say I've played at far worse grounds on the county circuit. The wicket was a little slow and I had to wait to play my shots. I hit a couple of sixes and I was pleased that I could maintain my concentration against bowling that wasn't quite as testing as Middlesex's. This game could've been a banana skin and we did well to come out of it like this.

DILLEY:

I didn't play in the end because there'd been a bit of a reaction to Lord's from my knee and I'd also gone in the back. Ten minutes before the toss-up I couldn't really move, so we decided to rest it for a county game. Playing a five-day Test is much worse than two county games on the trot, even though you get a rest on the Sunday. I sleep far easier during a county game, whereas it's much tougher on the nerves when you're playing for England. The tension gets to you and tires you. I wasn't really worried by the game at March – I thought we would be too professional for them and we were. A mediocre county side might have lost because it was cold, windy, with a threat of rain, and we were in unfamiliar territory. Their captain asked Phil Neale if he'd like to bat first but Phil refused. He wanted to win the game, even if it meant the crowd didn't see Botham and Hick bat. Even in a benefit game, Phil's like that: he wants to win the toss, put them in and win. That's the footballer in him – never give anyone a thing. Hicky played exactly the same way as he would against the best county bowlers. He won't be self-indulgent, he waits for the bad ball and plays straight. It was a very enjoyable day. Everyone at the ground was very hospitable and pleasant and it was a pleasure to sign a lot of autographs for so many polite people who clearly appreciated they were seeing a few big names on a rare visit. It actually took me back to my days in club cricket and that's never a bad thing.

So we've got Derbyshire at home in the next round. Nine times out of ten I'd prefer to play at home, but New Road seems such an intimidating place for our batters these days. If Michael Holding takes a fancy to the pitch, we might land in some strife, but we have to be happy with the draw. Perhaps Harry Brind's advice might have worked the oracle by 12 July.

RECOVERIES AND REVELATIONS

Worcestershire's players approached the start of July in determined mood. They knew that within another week the championship would be at the halfway mark and that some progress up the table had to be made now. Essex, still unbeaten, and Northants were beginning to pull away at the head of the table, and last year's champions were aware that form and luck must soon go their way if they were to have any chance of retaining the title. That gave the match at Northampton an extra edge when it started on 1 July. It turned out to be Worcestershire's best performance of the season so far — victory by an innings and 19 runs, coupled with a comfortable win by six wickets in the Sunday league game at Tring. They scored 433 against Northampton's 256 and 158. For Hick (111) and Dilley (4 for 66 in the second innings), it was also a personally satisfying weekend.

HICK:

It was hot, perfect weather for batting. When I first went in, I was keyed up. I wanted to play well against Curtley Ambrose because he's such a threat with his extra bounce, and the early stages were significant. Off the first ball – from Ambrose – I played a defensive shot off the back foot that raced away to the backward point boundary. I thought, 'That's not a bad piece of timing.' In his next over, I pushed forward and it went for four through extra cover. In just two balls I felt so much more confident, all my touch and timing seemed to return.

Nick Cook came on to bowl spin when I was getting into the 90s and we had an enjoyable contest. He had mid-off deep and wide and when he tossed one up I went down the pitch to hit him over long-on for six. I thought the next ball would either be the same or fired into my legs. It was another flighted ball – I got a little too close to it and hit it flat, about fifteen feet off the ground. The ball went past Cook before he saw it and smashed into the sight-screen first bounce, flat and hard. Next ball was again floated up and he nearly did me: it landed just in front of mid-off after I had mistimed it and I was grateful for a single. My bottom hand had slipped on the handle and I didn't time it right at all. I might have got out through over-confidence at that stage, and credit to the bowler for trying to get me out. In the end, Cook got me. He bowled it wide outside off-stump, I tried to run it down to third man instead of trying a hard cut and I nicked it to the keeper. That run-down shot is getting me out a lot this season. But I was satisfied that I'd got only my second championship hundred this season and played well. I feel this was something like I can play.

They've been pretty eventful days here in Northampton. When the match started on Saturday, Geoff Cook and Wayne Larkins smashed us all over the place. They'd got to 90 within the hour, but we were unlucky. Dill found the edge at least twice an over, but they kept edging him over the heads of the slips or through us for four. Then if he tried to york Larkins, he'd be whipped through mid-wicket. You have to pull back someone like Larkins before he gets too dominant and that's what he did. Beefy came on to bowl and took 6 wickets for 99, with variations of pace, and he showed a lot of stamina. I think we can safely assume he'll be picked for next week's Test now. He says that's no more than he deserves because he was fit for the last one, but never picked. He and Allan Lamb had a great duel, and after he'd been whacked a few times he did Lamby with an off-cutter and had him lbw. Then David Capel was seen off by Beefy, who always likes to put one over on the pretenders to his crown. Beefy was pumped up because he'd read some comments allegedly from Capel in a tabloid that it was time for Botham to move over. Capel was probably stuffed by the reporter – he doesn't seem the type to say such things – but that was all Beefy needed to get at him. Capel was almost caught first ball in the slips, hardly saw the second and off the fourth I caught him at slip. As Capel left, Beefy pointed out that they'd sent 'a boy to do a man's job'. I know it sounds ridiculous but when he gets fired up like that Beefy is still a hell of a cricketer.

I didn't particularly enjoy the Sunday game at Tring, apart from the victory by six wickets. The facilities were disappointing, and we had no privacy at all. People were passing our dressing-room window and even sitting down beside us outside. A professional sportsman needs a bit of time on his own to concentrate on his job during a game. Anyway we won, even if we made heavy weather of it. Nick Cook caught and bowled me, when I wasn't quite to the pitch of the ball, trying to push it for a single.

Next morning, the police are in our dressing room. Beefy was in the news again. A paper alleged he'd beaten up somebody at a pub near Northampton the night before and that he and Dennis Lillee had chased after him. We were very amused at the allegation and I cut out the headline and stuck it on the wall of his changing area. I'd just finished doing it when he walked in and smiled. He just seemed to be resigned to the story, but said it was complete rubbish. He said he and Lillee were standing at the hamburger stall in the pub when this guy smashed him in the face, and knocked him down. I can't understand what gets into these people, unless it's to brag about it to their mates or for money. If Ian Botham went to Zimbabwe, everyone would be so excited at seeing him that they'd enjoy him rather than pester him. He only wants to lead a normal life, but many won't let him.

Beefy was glad to get out into the middle away from the media attention, and in the second innings he again bowled well. At last he seems to have found an extra yard of pace so that he's hurrying the batters into the shot. He got Capel again and it was really funny. Capel was batting really well, creaming Beefy for a few boundaries, when he misjudged the length slightly and hit it straight to Phil Neale in the covers. That was enough for Beefy. 'Hit that one for four then!' he shouted at Capel and proceeded to tell us he'd deliberately held the ball back. We were certain he'd simply lost his run-up and delivered the ball slightly off-balance, but he believes what he wants. Anyway, he'd seen off Capel twice in the match and that meant a lot to him. I think Capel's a good batsman with a good technique, but although he works very hard at his bowling he seems to lack rhythm. Sometimes the ball seems to come out wrong and takes longer to get down the other end than when he's raced into the stumps. You still have to back Beefy ahead of him for the Tests this summer, if only for his self-belief and potential.

The most impressive piece of bowling in the match came from Dill. He really roared in on the final morning and it's the quickest I've seen from him. On a flat wicket, too. He'd been upset that one of their groundstaff had suggested that Dill had damaged the wicket with spikes when looking at it on the last morning. The captain closed our dressing-room door and asked if anyone was responsible. Everyone had gone to look at the pitch because two holes – one of them on a good length – were so noticeable. But no one had tampered with the wicket from our side. That really got Dill going. He was warned for bouncing Larkins and he just blasted through their batters. I'm sure his pace helped get Beefy a wicket or two at the other end as well, because none of them fancied it. David Ripley nicked one through the slips for four and it came through so quickly that none of us could get anywhere near it. We moved back a yard after that! He then bowled Ripley with a beautiful slower ball. Ripley had backed away, but then came back into line when he realised it wasn't going to be a quick one. He was done in the air and his off-stump was knocked back. Very intelligent bowling. When it was all over and we were about to have lunch, a lady in the dining room asked Dill if he'd like salad or braised steak. He asked for steak and then Jack Bond, one of the umpires, said 'Doesn't he want it raw?' He did look furious about the spiking incident and it was turned to our advantage because we won the game. That's pegged back Northants a bit. Now we must get on a winning roll.

DILLEY:

I was bloody annoyed at the slur. One ball had gone through the top on the second evening and we all went to look at it next morning. I lifted up the hole with my finger as we stood there, but at no time did I scuff it with my spikes. Anyway I wear rubbers when I bowl in the nets so the groundsman was talking through his backside. My anger didn't have an awful lot to do with me bowling fast, though. You just can't run up and bowl like that for over an hour because you're blazing mad. The wicket had flattened out after the first day and I felt we needed to give it a bit of a blast in the first hour. To get the ball quickly down the other end, I have to open up my body. When I'm trying to make it swing, my front foot is in line with my back foot, but when I go for sheer speed my left foot comes to about eleven o'clock on the dial, with my hips opened up early to allow me to push the ball through. I didn't swing it all today, I just opted for pace.

Wayne Larkins was the man to get out. I was warned by Roy Palmer the umpire for overdoing the bouncer but I ignored that. I didn't see why I should co-operate on a flat wicket in perfectly clear light. He'd just whacked me over mid-wicket a couple of times, so was I supposed to let him drive me off the front foot by pitching it up? In the space of a few minutes, I hit him on the shoulder, back and hand and that definitely reduced his fervour for the battle. I got what I wanted by ignoring the umpire. The law gives you a certain amount of leeway and I knew I'd used up all the leeway. It was psychologically important that their batters were disturbed to see their best batsmen in trouble through my hostility. You're not going to hurt anyone, but you want to make the batter physically unsure. There's no point in bouncing one three feet above his head, so I aim somewhere between the chest and nose. Ideally I'd like to aim at the batsman's head, see him glove it away in the nick of time and get caught at short leg without anyone being hurt.

I don't like hitting people. I broke Geoff Cook's jaw here at Northampton last year and I felt terrible because he's such a nice bloke. In my first Test, I hit Allan Border on the head and there was a fair amount of blood around. When I played in South Africa, the rugby section of my club side jokingly offered to sponsor me for a case of lager every time I drew blood on the wicket. I remember hitting Rob Bentley – a good friend of mine in Natal – when he hooked too early. The ball struck him straight in the mouth and he needed forty-two stitches. Things like that affect me. When I hit someone on the thigh or the arm and he starts rubbing it, I think 'I hope it hurts,' because from the neck downwards is fair game for the fast bowler, whose job is to unsettle batters. I do feel sorry for a guy who gets a broken finger, then struggles to get back in the first team after a month, but that's part and parcel of the game. Fast bowlers are the bullies, and without an awareness of physical danger the batsmen would love to keep driving us off the front foot all day.

I was just getting revenge for the tonking I took in that first innings. One for 90 off nineteen overs isn't exactly the best preparation for next week's Test, but I honestly bowled quite well. I must have beaten the bat about thirty times, yet they kept nicking me to the boundary, then despatching every loose ball. I just had to calm down and accept it, even though I was sometimes going for ten an over. Cook and Larkins have been a very good opening pair over the last decade. I would say that only Paul Terry and Gordon Greenidge have been a better pair in county cricket in my time – and only then when Gordon was concentrating. Cook is the sensible one of the two. If you bowl him three bad balls on the trot, he'll hit them for four, then block the fourth if it's a good ball. Wayne would try to smash the fourth after getting twelve runs off three shots. Wayne's a bit of a cameo man, but very talented. He came on my first England tour to Australia and India in 1979/80 and he didn't actually apply himself. I can see him even now in Sydney, sauntering down to the team bus after a good night at the Bourbon and Beefsteak Bar. That didn't go down too well with the hierarchy, despite his great natural ability, and that tour set him back. I suspect his England chances have gone now, and that's a pity.

It was a good effort to peg them back on Saturday after such a spectacular start, but Northants are like that, more than any other side. They go to pieces after a flier quite often, they play too many shots and do surrender domination. That's why I don't think they'll be a danger in the championship, despite their good start this year.

So Beefy makes the front pages again for another little encounter. Much as I like and respect the bloke, I can't help thinking at such times, 'Bloody hell, what's he done now?' We'd left the pub earlier, but apparently Beefy is completely innocent this time. It doesn't worry me to see police in our dressing room. Our young lads think it's a good laugh and a bit of a novelty, but when you've seen Elton John and Eric Clapton in our dressing room, a police inspector's no big deal. Beefy certainly cast his shadow over this match in one way or another. He bowled with heart and stamina on Saturday, got picked for England and had his face punched on Sunday, got run out for nought on Monday and bowled very well again on Tuesday morning. When he was run out – Phil Neale's drive was deflected by the bowler on to the stumps at Beefy's end – he came back with a grin on his face. I think he'd rather curse his luck like that than be out for nought with his off-pole knocked out by David Capel. This rivalry with Capel brings out his competitive streak and he doesn't want to be beaten on ability. It's hard to compare two blokes of differing characters but I get the feeling that, if the roles were reversed, Capel wouldn't have overwhelmed Botham in four balls, as Botham overwhelmed him on Saturday. Beefy is mentally so strong.

Hicky's hundred was a high-class effort. When he came in, I was watching from the dressing room and someone said, 'Bloody hell, he's blocked that one for four!' off Ambrose's first ball. He's such a beautiful timer. Again Tim Curtis supported him in a large stand. They are the backbone of our side as batters and I believe TC does as good a job as Graeme in terms of his basic ability. He does tremendously well to get so many runs every season. Today we've learned that he's been called up by England for the Edgbaston Test (more injuries!) and I hope he does very well. I'm a little worried though that he needs a bigger ego to succeed in Test cricket. After the pundits slated him for his technique against the West Indies last year, he came back to Worcester confused, and started to experiment with his bat on the floor, rather than raised. That was daft. If he'd thought there was genuinely room for improvement, Tim should've waited for the winter nets to work at it, not during a season when you can be batting almost every day. I hope Tim doesn't get too tense at Edgbaston – he must learn to relax for the big games, otherwise he won't be able to function properly. His feet won't be able to go where he wants them to go when he's tense. It's true Tim plays across the line of the ball a little, but the batsman's prime objective is to hit the ball. So when the ball jags back into him, he has to play slightly across the line and the front pad to get to the ball. If he came down straight, he'd miss it by a mile.

Anyway a satisfactory, action-packed trip to Northampton. From a personal point of view, I bowled my fastest this season and my control was also good in the second innings. It's put me in better heart for Edgbaston than I was for Lord's. From a team point of view, we needed a win because we can't leave it too much later for our charge.

Hick and his team-mates returned to Worcester while Dilley travelled twenty-five miles to Edgbaston for the Third Test. The local derby against Warwickshire proved an interesting match with some fine individual performances (particularly Smith's 140 for Warwickshire), but it was drawn after torrential thunderstorms. Essex, Lancashire and Northants suffered in the same way, so that by the halfway stage of the championship season Worcestershire lay in fourth place, thirty-four points behind the leaders, Essex, with the same number of games played. For Worcestershire's match with Warwickshire, a significant decision had been taken.

🏏 HICK:

We're going to use the Tworts ball from now on and I think that's a wise move. The Reader ball never seems to lose its seam and it's lively all the time. At least with the Tworts ball you've got a chance of getting in if the ball gets softer. Then you only have to worry about the wicket! But I think it makes sense to switch, with the risk of a twenty-five points deduction still around. No point in making things harder for ourselves with the Reader ball as well.

We went into this Warwickshire game with a depleted side, but it's been encouraging to see the stand-ins take their chance. We've lost Botham, Dilley and Curtis to the Test and Phil Newport has broken down again with Achilles troubles. He's been troubled by it since the Leeds Test and it looks like a long job. That's a real blow because Newps has taken so many wickets for us this season and in other years. With our bowling looking a little threadbare, we might now have to rely on our batting to chase a few targets. But you never know: Steve McEwan has come in from the seconds for this game and bowled very well. He's been on the scene for some years now and he looks very keen to make up for lost time. He's twenty-seven now, about to get married, so it's an important period in his career – make or break really. He bowls straight, is quick enough to slip in a bouncer and because he's comparatively new on the scene he might surprise a few. He skips a little in his run-up and you think his rhythm must be all wrong, but the ball gets down the other end sharply enough. Steve also got some runs – he and Stuart Lampitt added 72 for the last wicket and they both got their best scores in first-class cricket. I think Lampitt is a very talented all-rounder and he's very keen to get a first-team place. Both are very hungry and that could just be the kind of attitude we need.

Richard Illingworth is also hungry. He took 4 wickets for 33 in their innings and that was worth another celebratory hamburger. Illy has increased the sales of McDonald's dramatically in the Worcester area. He also loves his chips – when we're batting he often sneaks around to the other side of the ground for a burger and chips. When he drops a catch in the field, we say, 'You'd have caught that if it was a cheeseburger!' Underneath the banter, we have great respect for Illy as an underrated spinner, brave short leg and reliable nightwatchman. This season he's at last starting to give the ball more air and Steve Rhodes is picking up a stumping or two off him. One of his nicknames is 'Lucy', after 'Lucifer', because he's a bit of a devil on the field. A typical Yorkshireman, he growls and snarls on the pitch, loves to throw the ball back hard at the keeper when his over is finished and lets the batters know he doesn't think much of them. But he gives us everything. With all these injuries about – and Test calls – Illy could have a lot of bowling ahead of him.

In our only innings, I was bowled by Tony Merrick for 4, playing back to a ball that came in a fair way and took my off-stump. I should've played forward on a pitch of such variable bounce. My defence wasn't good enough. It struck me during the game that I was now a senior player in our side. Stu Lampitt is only two months younger than me and Steve McEwan is four years older, but in terms of experience I am far older. I must now start thinking more and more like a senior player because the captain needs support from us. He can't be expected to be as successful with a new-look unit like this one unless players like me are coming through with suggestions and advice. It's a strange feeling, being so young and yet comparatively so experienced.

While wickets were clattering on yet another eventful first day at New Road in the Warwickshire match, Dilley checked in at Edgbaston with the rest of the England side for the Third Test. The build-up was hardly conventional.

━━▶ DILLEY:

I can't believe the bad luck we're having. First we lose Robin Smith and Allan Lamb through injuries, now we find that Neil Foster is doubtful with a blistered finger on his bowling hand. Worst of all, Mike Gatting has had to pull out because his mother-in-law died suddenly this afternoon. That was an awful moment: Gatt was in the dressing room telling us that she hadn't been very well lately and that they hadn't been able to get the doctor out to see her, when he decided to phone home. When he got through to his wife, he was told her mother had just died of a heart attack. How dreadful. I know the family well. They were all very fond of Elaine's mother, who lived with them and acted as Gatt's manager. I told Gatt to ring me any time if he ever needed to talk. He was very distressed. He's had a hell of a year.

So Chris Tavaré has been called up in a hurry. It was lovely to see him again, although not in these circumstances. I reminded his wife Vanessa that she owed me a lot of pocket money – she used to mother me during our early days at Kent. I said to Tav, 'What the hell are you doing here?' and he smiled and said, 'I don't know.' Actually it's a good move. When Gatt left for London we took a straw poll in the dressing room for his replacement and a few went for Tav. I suggested we should cancel the rest of the series and wait till Graeme Hick was available in 1991! But if you had to put your money on anyone to shore up the England batting it would be the Chris Tavaré I knew at Kent. Nowadays at Somerset he plays a bit freer but he's got such a great temperament that I don't believe he'll struggle against these Aussies. He's such a great team man.

I admired the quiet, brave way he tackled the problems of favouritism at Kent. He took on the huge job of trying to put our cricket on a professional basis, trying to rewrite Kent's history. But the lure of the Cowdrey name did Tav in the end and he was out. They chose Chris Cowdrey as captain because they said Tav lacked charisma on the field. But you don't need to run around, clapping your hands for attention, smacking the boys on the back. Tav had the automatic respect of the players, he only needed to nod his head because everyone looked at him on the field. He has a brilliant cricket brain and if Kent hadn't sacked him and he hadn't played so badly against Sri Lanka in 1984, he would've gone to India as vice-captain to David Gower – and then what?

I'm puzzled about Neil Foster's problem. We all get blistered fingers if we bowl enough overs. It did look a deep one but he seems very negative about it. You would've thought that a guy who's come through all his back and knee injuries wouldn't be fazed by something like this. Paul Jarvis is standing by and I'm pleased for him, because he needs a settled run in the side to give of his best.

We're staying at the Plough and Harrow, about a mile and a half from the ground, and very nice it is too. It's a vital part of preparation for a Test at home that you should feel comfortable in your hotel. We get down on tour in hotels and I think you should spoil yourself if you're playing for your country at home. At our team dinner David Gower seemed a touch more tense than usual. He emphasised all the obvious points and we knew that we were in a desperate situation, so there was no need to bang on about it. The bowlers admitted they hadn't done their job well enough, while at least we had to acknowledge that the batters had got a few hundreds at Leeds and Lord's. It was a case of diminishing optimism but we still had to tell ourselves we were as good as them. None of the players bound for South Africa had much to say to each other, apart from checking there was no hard news about the time when the story would break. I've opened negotiations with Western Province to play out there and I asked the advice of Graham Gooch. I don't know if Goochy's signed up for the tour – it's a personal matter and I wouldn't dream of asking him.

One laugh at the team dinner. Fozzie and I had a bet that Ian Botham would say that none of the Aussie batsmen like the bouncer – his stock forecast at every team meeting I've attended when he's been around. David went through all their players and not once did Beefy mention the bouncer. Significantly he was positive in a more constructive way – saying that we hadn't put enough pressure on them by bowling tightly, that occupation of the crease was the way to blunt Alderman. All that was totally alien to what Beefy has stood for in the past, with all his over-the-top stuff. Either he's not very confident about his own form or he's come to terms with the fact that he can't run in and bowl quick bouncers any more. We shall see.

Day One – Australia 232/4 (Jones 71 not out).

DILLEY:

Not much chance of glory here. It looks a good wicket and the weather is uncertain. Tonight we had the most amazing thunderstorm I've seen in this country. Unless there's a dramatic change, we're looking down the barrel of at least 350 from the Aussies and reduced time to do anything about it. The ground was a little wet when we started this morning. I'm sure that if we'd been two-up in the series we'd have been happy to sit in the dressing room, but we need every one of the thirty hours available. We also didn't get any luck. How Paul Jarvis didn't win an lbw shout in his first over to Geoff Marsh I will never know. Jack Russell said it was out – keepers usually are the best judges – and this evening I've watched it on the TV highlights and it was bloody plumb. I'm becoming concerned about umpiring standards in Tests in this country. Some of our umpires are reckoned to be the best in the world, yet more and more they seem to be not-outers. If you're a not-outer that helps to get you on to the Test panel and that makes you more money. Everybody in the England dressing room has felt this for some time. Our umpires – unlike those of other countries – seem to bend over backwards to be fair, and as a result the visitors appear to get the benefit of the doubt.

Today we desperately needed an early breakthrough to put them under pressure but they got to lunch without losing a wicket and then it was just a case of containing them. John Emburey bowled very well – he seems more relaxed – and Jack Russell's stumping off him to get Mark Taylor was a fine piece of team-work. Angus Fraser impressed me greatly on his first day as an England bowler. It's very hard to run up and do what you do in the county game right from the start but he did. He seemed different from the other young seamers around – he's quiet, sensible and ignores the no-balls. Talent involves bowling to your strengths and using common sense as well as your natural ability, and to me Gus already has the Test-match temperament. Beefy bowled well in a containing role, but we needed the old Botham to run in and blast a few out. But there was no one at the other end to do the containing role like Mike Hendrick and Chris Old used to do for him.

Paul Jarvis and I were going for four an over again. I started with a reasonable spell but I lost it after that and just got worse and worse. Dean Jones kept hitting me through mid-wicket and I thought that meant I was straying down leg-side. Now I've watched the highlights I see he's hitting me off middle and off! That takes a hell of an eye and timing. I thought he'd struggle on English wickets because he plays like this, but I suppose we're just not bowling well enough at him. He's one of those blokes you want to see embarrassed on the field because he's so irritating, he's full of himself – always practising shots after he's hit you for four, and he's a real strutter around the place. He's just not used to the ups and downs of daily professional cricket like we are. I hope we weren't as insufferable when we did so well in Australia a couple of years back. These Aussies are sauntering around here as if they own Edgbaston. Last time we played them, they were surly and unapproachable because things weren't going their way. I like to think we'll never get like that. I only wish we could ram their cockiness back down their throats. I know this is just my frustration coming out here, but I can't help an irrational annoyance at them, with our hopes going down the tube so disappointingly.

Day Two – Australia 294/6 (Jones 101 not out).

DILLEY:

A bloody awful day. For the team and for me. I bowled a load of crap, too much that was short outside off-stump – buffet bowling we call it, help-yourself stuff. I didn't lack effort or concentration – I kept telling myself I hadn't suddenly become a bad bowler, but it was very depressing. When a fast bowler gets smashed all over the park, he really has to work hard at hanging on to his rhythm. The bully is getting stuffed and there is never much sympathy around for the fast bowler at this time because often enough he calls the tune and intimidates the batsmen. So I just take my punishment and can feel the confidence draining out of me. Only Gus Fraser bowled properly and at last he got Steve Waugh out. He's a fine player but he's no Bradman – he's not even a Chappell. We should be bowling good-length balls on or just outside his off-stump (Micky Stewart's channel), but we're giving him too much room to play his shots. Why are we incapable of pausing at the start of our run-ups and telling ourselves what kind of ball the batter will get? We can only blame ourselves. Their batsmen are being allowed to bat well. The only light relief from the day was before we went out at last around tea-time. We sat and watched some of the old Ashes games on the TV and it's an odd feeling to see yourself on the screen from all those years ago. I'm proud to turn up on screen so often in partnership with Beefy during his amazing innings at Leeds in 1981, but we all know that you should never compare different players and different series with the current one. We don't do that but the media kept expecting Botham to turn on the tap after all this time.

Day Three – Australia 391/7 (Jones 141 not out).

DILLEY:

We're up the creek. The best we can hope for is another draw and then the miracles have to start in the remaining three Tests. Starting on Monday we have to score around 600, then bowl them out for next to nothing – all in the space of 180 overs. Impossible, even if Terry Alderman slips in the shower. We mustn't give up though, otherwise we'll lose again. We just have to make it difficult for them on Monday and Tuesday. Just thirty-one overs were bowled today and a depressing experience it was for all of us, apart from the excellent Gus Fraser. I've topped the hundred in this innings and so I should. I've just bowled worse in each new spell. I'm really disappointed, because I was hoping for a good series before I said farewell to England. I want to get up the list of all-time Test wicket-takers. I'd started the series with 133 and I was aiming for Tony Greig's 141 and then to go on from there. I want people to say how much I'll be missed when I go to South Africa, but at the moment no one's going to shed any tears at my departure.

Sunday, 9 July – rest day.

⊏⊐▬ DILLEY:

I don't feel terribly restful. I feel at the end of my tether at the moment. I'm getting worn down by the South African thing. I've turned down an offer of £10,000 by a tabloid newspaper to reveal that I've been approached and, although that was no problem, I do wish the story would soon come out into the open. I like to be totally frank with people who I like and, if it came out, then David Gower could decide whether he wants us in the side or not. Everyone's talking about South Africa at the moment and, although I'm not close with many in the media, I know that they'll be putting us under a lot of pressure from now on. I shan't break my promise of silence to Ali Bacher but I wonder if everyone else will keep quiet.

Mike Brearley's had a little dart at me today in the *Sunday Times*. He writes, 'The big question-mark, after all these years, lies over Dilley's will.' Does it really? Mike was my first England captain but I've had no contact at all with him for years. I appreciate even the quality papers want their men to write a certain way but I think Mike is a little out of touch about me. I don't know what I have to do to show my willingness. When I was young and showed more aggression on the field, they said my temperament wasn't sound enough. Now, because I don't stand there with hands on hips, shouting abuse at batsmen, I'm supposed to be lacking the will. That's rubbish. In every aspect of life you work out what you want to do and how you go about it. I realised I had my own inhibitions and way of approaching my bowling and that's what I've settled on. I bloody well know that I'm bowling badly for England this year, but that's got nothing at all to do with willpower.

Day Four – Australia 424 (Jones 157), England 185/7.

DILLEY:

More flak coming our way, I suppose. We're still 40 short of avoiding the follow-on, but it's a flat wicket and even if we do have to bat again we should get away with it. But why are the Aussies dictating to us with bat and ball? Of course, Terry Alderman bowled well (again), but we're allowing them to get into a situation where they can stick two men close in on the leg-side to Graham Gooch. They have all these runs in hand – if they'd been out for 224 they wouldn't have been able to afford to have two men in there for so many overs because runs would be coming elsewhere. Gooch was lbw again and I feel sorry for him. You only have to talk to our umpires about people like Alderman and Hadlee to realise why they win so many lbw appeals. They say, 'Oh, they get so close to the stumps that it must be near if they ever hit the pad.' It's on their minds straightaway: even if it pitches outside the off-stump or it's simply going straight on, the umpires are subconsciously influenced. Now our batters are dreading putting their front up the wicket, so they're playing more at the ball than they want to when it's anywhere near the off-stump. Terry Alderman is no Dennis Lillee – he's a fine, thoughtful bowler who bowls straight. There's no reason why we can't blunt him if we play to our strengths. Perhaps the West Indies are right – they

111

say he can't bowl to them because they get after him and disrupt his line.

Beefy batted well though for his 46. It was set up for him when he came in, with England in desperate straits, and he batted responsibly. It reminded me of the Test at the Oval two years ago when he blocked it out against Pakistan. He couldn't believe it when Merv Hughes bowled him with a straight one. He doesn't think Merv can bowl, and he was done by an inside edge. I thought he might have gone on to a hundred. That would've been textbook stuff, to keep the legend going.

Day Five – England 242, Australia 158/2. Match drawn.

DILLEY:

This was a day like they used to have in five-day Tests, when the wickets were better and a draw was the only objective from a long way out. We avoided the follow-on, thanks to a last-wicket stand between Paul Jarvis and myself. I enjoyed my innings and I felt so comfortable that Graham Gooch said in the dressing room, 'Dill's in no trouble out there – he could play it with a stick of rhubarb!' I'd worked out a method of batting against them. I knew that Lawson would either angle it across me or bowl it short, so he was no problem. As for Alderman, I didn't commit myself to anything around off-stump. I waited for him to bowl straight and then tried to tuck him off my legs. It worked. Then another frustrating umpiring decision when Jarvo was given out, lbw to Alderman. That was another one for Terry's reputation. It wasn't hitting any stumps and I also think Jarvo nicked the ball. If that was out, then so was Marsh on the first day. To me it looked a case of 'Okay, you've done your job, you've saved the follow-on, so off you go.' There was no thread of consistency.

So ends another depressing Test. We haven't performed well again and we are now running out of time and the materials to build a recovery. Angus Fraser looked very impressive on his début, Jack Russell again batted with spirit and John Emburey bowled as well as he's done for England for some time. Apart

Graeme Hick.

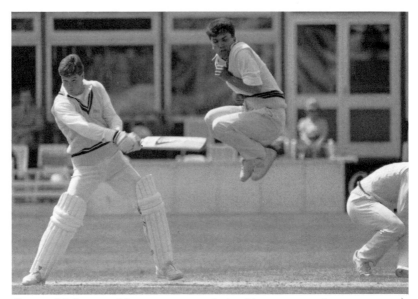

Graeme Hick cuts with savage power during his century against
Northampton. Nigel Felton is the fielder wishing he was somewhere
else.

Worcestershire face the media on arrival at Brisbane in April on their
pre-season tour. Inevitably most of the questions are directed at Graeme
Hick: will he be playing for Queensland later in the year?

Graham Dilley.

Contrasting emotions for Graham Dilley in the Lord's Test against Australia:
twice beating the bat, concentration – and then joy.

Graeme Hick's developing off-spin was an important bowling option as the wickets got drier in late season. Umpire David Constant seems impressed.

The push through mid-wicket that brings so many boundaries to Graeme Hick.

Ian Botham and Graham Hick: the two great entertainers in Worcestershire's batting line-up – but they have rarely batted together.

Ian Botham, Graeme Hick and Steve Rhodes celebrate another slip catch.

Graham Dilley appears in the unaccustomed position of first slip alongside the experts, Ian Botham and Graeme Hick.

Worcestershire clinch the championship title after beating Gloucestershire at home. Graham Dilley leads the way.

Graham Dilley accepts the plaudits of team-mates after winning the championship. The supporting shoulders are those of the team's wicket keeper, Steve Rhodes.

Phil Neale accepts a cheque for £37,000 to mark Worcestershire's triumphant retention of the county championship. A proud club chairman, Duncan Fearnley is to the left of the captain.

Champagne for Graeme Hick as the championship is secured for the second year in a row.

Graham Dilley is introduced to the Duke of Edinburgh by Worcestershire's president, Don Kenyon, at Buckingham Palace at the presentation of the Lord's Taverners Trophy in November. To Dilley's left are Gordon Lord, Steve Rhodes and Paul Pridgeon, who reflects on a happy occasion to mark his final season with Worcestershire.

from that – nothing. It's a case of scuttling off with the tail between the legs, hoping that Joe Public doesn't give us too hard a time on the way to our cars and keeping the head down. Glamorous life, isn't it?

Graeme Hick enjoyed those few days rather more. Worcestershire played Leicestershire at Kidderminster, the club where Hick had started his English career, breaking all records in two years before he qualified for the county. Worcestershire continued to advance on the leading pack in two competitions, thrashing Leicestershire by ten wickets in the championship and by six wickets in the Refuge.

⊜ HICK:

They didn't offer us too much resistance in either game. Even at this stage of the season they look as if they're going through the motions and they ought to have done better than 80 all out in the second innings. The wicket at Kidderminster is always a very good one, as I remember with great pleasure, but for some reason the games we play here are always over early with a few low scores. It's a very good cricket wicket, with the ball coming on to the bat and the bowlers getting some encouragement as well. Yet I don't seem to get many runs here for Worcestershire. In the championship game, I dragged one on from Gordon Parsons after playing well, then on Sunday Dolly ran me out. That was just a mix-up, one of those 'yes, no' situations, but I'm a little bothered about the number of times I'm playing on this season. The ball came back a little off the seam and I got an inside edge going for the drive. Possibly I'm not getting my foot far enough over for the off-drive to a wide ball. More work in the nets! But I do believe that if you want to hit the ball hard you have to get your arms free of the body and that means getting your foot out of the way to let the ball come through. Some fine tuning needed here.

Steve Rhodes played a gutsy innings to pull us round after we'd slumped to 130 for 8 on Monday, still 40-odd behind. He and Richard Illingworth added 79, then Steve McEwan also hung around for valuable time and runs. That's the kind of performance which wins games and titles, and Leicestershire could never follow that. Steve McEwan bustled in and took nine wickets in the match. He seems to be able to find that gap between bat and pad against batsmen who haven't seen all that much of him. If he can keep picking up wickets like this, that'll give us a major boost as we chase Essex.

There was one time in this game when I was perfectly happy for rain to stop play. On Saturday afternoon, we were able to sit in the clubhouse and watch a fantastic five-setter at Wimbledon between Boris Becker and Ivan Lendl. I've been a couple of times to Wimbledon and I can appreciate the speed and athleticism involved. I automatically side with Becker because he's young and successful, but I did feel sorry for Lendl. It seems he's fated never to win Wimbledon.

Wednesday, 12 July – Worcestershire 278/7 (Botham 53, Rhodes 61) beat Derbyshire (240) by 38 runs in the NatWest Cup.

HICK:

There's bound to be some talk that I dropped down from number three to four but today it made sense. It was a humid morning and obviously Michael Holding would be quite a test once they'd decided to put us in. The first hour was going to be vital. Phil Neale felt that the pitch would be a little damp early on and that Steve Rhodes would be ideal at defending correctly and scampering quick singles to disrupt their rhythm and field-placings. The captain asked me what I thought and I said I was quite happy to stay where I was, but that I could see the sense of what he was saying. On the one hand I didn't want to run away from the challenge, but I also thought that for once it would be nice to face the ball when it was slightly older. This time it worked. Steve played superbly for his 61 and I got a quick 45 before Holding had me caught behind as I tried to nudge a single. I'd thought about going down the wicket to him because he had both mid-on and mid-off up, but his line and length were so good that you couldn't take liberties against him. But we got a good start and it was set up for one of Beefy's specials. He hit a couple of enormous sixes and the crowd loved it. We've missed having him accelerate like this after a good start – it seems the middle order has had to rebuild an innings for most of this summer. He then built on his batting by bowling intelligently and keeping it tight when they were looking to get on with it. The ball to get John Morris was a fine one. Morris, a dangerous player, went forward to play the perfect defensive stroke and the ball clipped the top of the off-stump. No prizes for guessing the Man of the Match award, though Steve Rhodes was just as important on the day.

DILLEY:

I'm sure Derbyshire will admit they lost this game because they dropped too many catches in the morning when we were struggling in the humid conditions and against good bowling. But I thought we played well and it was good to see Beefy take a game by the scruff of the neck and turn it his way. He was brought here to entertain crowds and help us win trophies and I reckon he's fulfilling his part of the bargain. I wasn't over-keen on Graeme dropping down the order. He's our best player and more than capable of fighting it out. If he bats for fifty-five overs rather than forty-five, that's at least another 50 runs from the Hick bat. Phil Neale surprised me in two ways. The way he smashed the ball around in the slog overs was a real eye-opener. Before I came here, I wouldn't have believed him capable of such unorthodoxy. He also kept faith with Stu Lampitt in the closing overs when Derbyshire were chasing the target. I've been told that Stuey is the best bowler at the death in the seconds and Phil obviously had faith in him. It's indicative of our team spirit that he kept him on when they only needed 80 off the last ten overs and Radford and I still had a few in hand. Stuey did very well. He bowled a full length and with his fast arm he gets away with it because he's quicker than he looks. That was an encouraging performance from him. Stuey could be very useful to us in the next few weeks when injuries pile up with all these fixtures to play.

As usual Michael Holding bowled well but I'm sorry to say that things won't be the same between us again. He's jumped on the media bandwagon and he got stuck into me in a tabloid for my performance at Edgbaston. Somehow I find that harder to take from someone who's retired from Tests but is still playing county cricket. By choice I'd never slag off a fellow-professional in print. Obviously Michael's forgotten how difficult this game can be or perhaps he needs the money. Michael likes a bet on the horses. I've always got on well with him but I'll just be polite to him in the future.

Dilley continued to go through a bad patch, both on and off the field. Worcestershire had to reprimand him for a gesture during the game to Reg Sharma. Dilley had appeared to point to the pavilion dismissively. The *Independent* said the incident involved 'Yet another of those silly Dilley gestures, which emphasise his juvenile mind and do his team no credit at all.'

DILLEY:

Mike Vockins, our secretary, had a word about it and he was right to do so. I explained the background – that I don't see eye to eye with Reg Sharma, after spending our early days together playing in Kent – but Mike was correct in saying that what people saw was more relevant than the underlying tensions between us. Others do it all the time – look at Merv Hughes, look at Beefy to Capel at Northampton – but all those wrongs don't make a right. It was low-key and typically sensible of the secretary.

On a brighter note, we've drawn Lancashire at home in the next round of the NatWest. They're the best side still left in the competition, apart from us, but we're playing so much better now than when they beat us early in May. The wicket played quite well yesterday – it was slow and low – and if we have a similar one for the Lancashire game, we should win.

Meanwhile the South African saga picked up extra momentum with the news that Ali Bacher and Joe Pamensky, representing the South African Cricket Union, had been refused permission to speak to the International

Cricket Conference on the progress towards multi-racial cricket in South Africa. It now seemed inevitable that an unofficial England tour would go ahead in the winter.

DILLEY:

It would've made no difference anyway if they'd got in to address the meeting because people's minds were already made up. Ali Bacher only wanted them to come over, have a look and see how things have changed, but political matters are clearly at work here. The white governing body of cricket in South Africa is doing everything possible to make cricket multi-racial, as I know from personal experience. At some stage the ICC will sit down and listen to what Ali has to say. I'd have more respect for those running world cricket if they'd officially listened, then made up their minds not to go to South Africa, instead of slamming the door. It's just playing into the hands of those who want rebel tours.

On Saturday, 15 July, Worcestershire trekked up to Scarborough, for a Sunday league game the following day. En route, Dilley spared a thought for an old friend.

DILLEY:

I listened to the Benson and Hedges final on the car radio between Essex and Nottinghamshire and I really felt for John Lever when Eddie Hemmings hit him for four to win the game off the last ball. Steve Rhodes was in the car with me as John prepared to deliver the last ball and I said, 'My mortgage is on JK.' But Hemmings squirted him to the third-man boundary. I knew that JK would take it well, giving a little sigh as he headed for the pavilion, but I bet he was close to tears. I've never seen him get upset – he handles himself well and is tremendously popular. He's been a great pro, and he and I got on well together right away on my first England tour. When he coached me in South Africa, he did more for me on the mental side than anyone else before. He made me aware of what I should be doing as a professional out on the field, that you don't just bowl your overs, bugger off to third man and have a bit of a doze. You have to keep looking at what the batsmen are trying to do, assess their footwork, what shots they don't play. He said you must always be ready with a suggestion to your captain and that's always been the Essex way. It's now the Worcestershire way as well. I just wish that JK had won that match, his last final at Lord's before he retires.

Around 10,000 crammed into Scarborough's ground to see Worcestershire win by six wickets off the last ball. Chasing 205 in forty overs, Botham and Curtis added 138 for the first wicket, but their good start was almost wasted.

🏏 HICK:

We made an easy victory look very hard. When I finally got in, I needed a bit of time to adjust to the pitch and got bogged down. Dolly and I then got ourselves out, hitting the ball straight up in the air and Tim Curtis was caught at long-on. Phil Neale had to come in and hit the last ball of the game for four to win it and he was annoyed with us, especially as we still hoped to win the Sunday league. The captain was right: it was a rather dozy effort.

🏏 DILLEY:

It did us no harm at all to be bollocked by Phil in the dressing room. Such criticisms come rarely from Phil and that's also right because a captain shouldn't whinge all the time at his players. I got some hammer in my eight overs and so did Beefy, but that'll always happen on a Sunday to someone. It would be a fairer competition if you reduced it to thirty overs a side and then bowl up to six overs off proper run-ups, rather than a maximum twenty-two yards. Then we'd see just how brave people are when they start running down the pitch at you. At the moment I just run up and hope on Sundays.

I like the Yorkshire players and feel sorry for them with all those fanatics up there. The talent is there but they need a world-class batsman and overseas bowler to win them a championship. And God knows if they'll ever agree to that. I wouldn't like to play in front of that lot all the time. The ground at Scarborough has poor facilities, a small changing room and a trickle of water from the two showers, but what really gets to me is the way the spectators treat players. You desperately hope you can field first, so they're not too drunk and ready to abuse you. After tea, all you get is 'Piss off back down south' when you're fielding in front of them down on the boundary. Luckily I managed to stay inside the circle today – the dodgy knee meant I couldn't lope around the boundary with my customary fluency.

By now Harry Brind had carried out his early examination of the New Road square and he had recommended continuing the reconstruction over the next three years. He had also agreed to prepare personally a wicket for some county games before the end of the season at Worcester.

DILLEY:

That's helped us. We can now say to the TCCB, 'Your man's here on the spot, he knows how determined we are to get it right.' We might have been a candidate to lose twenty-five points if we hadn't been keen to do something about our pitches this season. Harry Brind's advice is going to be vital in helping us to solve what seems to be an inherent problem. It can't help that the square gets flooded so often in the winter. I suppose wickets also get tired and need to be dug up. But our home pitches have definitely affected us more than the opposition. We've lost eight games in all competitions so far this year – and seven of them have been at New Road. Our batters have been looking for demons and even we bowlers acknowledge that you do need to score runs to win matches.

On Tuesday, 19 July, Worcestershire travelled up to Manchester for a very important championship match against Lancashire, one of their main rivals for the title. At the very least they had to avoid defeat at the start of a month of almost continuous first-team cricket. Losing to Lancashire would be a heavy psychological blow, with so much high-pressure cricket to come in the space of a few weeks.

Day One – Worcestershire 191 (Neale 62), Lancashire 125 (Dilley 5/30).

HICK:

An action-packed day on the quickest wicket I've yet played on in England. Quite a few of us were hit. DeFreitas hit me on the head from the second ball I faced: I saw it coming as it pitched but then I just lost it. Welcome to Old Trafford! My reactions were a little slow because you just don't see wickets like this in England, but I soon got used to leaving the ball or getting out of the way. Patterson may have looked impressive as he bounced us, but he should have bowled it a couple of feet closer to us, because we had time to duck. Paul Allott got me on 21 off his first ball as I pushed forward to get a nick to second slip, standing a long way back. We would've been in trouble without Phil Neale and Dill. The captain has his own method of dealing with quick bowling that involves stepping back and giving himself room to cut. It may look as if he doesn't fancy the quicks but he gets in line when playing defensively. You don't see his stumps go cartwheeling all that often. Dill played really well at the end of the innings for his 31. Their bowlers were getting tired and they pitched it up more to him – because they knew that he can give it back if they bounce him – but he still picked up valuable runs with well-timed shots off his legs. He must be the best number eleven in the county game. When he came back to the dressing room he said, 'I don't know what's up with you lot, nobody can get me out!'

But he really made his mark with the ball this evening. When we were batting, they were very chirpy as the wickets kept falling. They loved it when Patterson kept bouncing us, but when Dill tore into them their smiles soon disappeared. He shot out the first three for just 5, bowling straight and fast. Some of their batters just didn't fancy it all and we felt we had played with more guts today. There was an edge between the two sides that made for a really tense atmosphere. When Patterson came in to bat this evening, Steve Rhodes was really pumped up behind the stumps, shouting out, 'Go on, Picca, give him what he gave us.' Patto looked round at Steve, bouncing around and shouting, and said to Beefy, 'I want him.' Could be an interesting second innings!

◁▭ DILLEY:

This has been a satisfying day, but a very long one. It was gone eight o'clock before we finished and I blame Lancashire for that. Their over rate was unbelievable – by lunch they'd only bowled twenty-five overs. I agree that the fall of nineteen wickets and treatment to injured batsmen takes up a fair amount of time but they took an eternity to bowl an over. You go into lunch thinking, 'I'd better have a good stoke up here, we'll be on the pitch till half-eight,' and that wasn't too far out. Patterson bowled an awful lot that was too short. He seemed to enjoy seeing his keeper leap up to get the ball. But that meant it wasn't too difficult for our batters to spot if it was going to be a full-length ball or a harmless bouncer, quick though he undoubtedly is. Phil Neale played brilliantly, getting inside the ball and carving it away. A batsman needed guts to stay out there, because he always expected to be hit. I managed to get runs because I'm tall and can get out of the way of bouncers and also through my experience of quick wickets abroad. When you've been hit on the wrist by Jeff Thomson at Perth, Patrick Patterson at Old Trafford isn't a great worry. I got runs by using the pace of the wicket for nudges and deflections. I drove the balls of full length and used the flick off my legs I'd pinched from Chris Broad. That one eventually got me out, but never mind. I didn't play the hook shot, though!

So we had something to bowl at and this evening I turned in my best effort of the season. They didn't fancy it after Fairbrother got an edge on to his helmet to be caught at short leg. He was helped off the field and the others didn't seem to want to know. I ran up to bowl short of a length at their rib cages and they jabbed out the catches. It was important for us to get a decent lead and to let them know that we could match Patterson for speed and hostility. We could give it back – and a little more besides. It's a great cricket wicket, the kind I'd like to play on all the time. I don't think this game is going to go the full distance and I'm certain they're not going to win it. We've got them by the throat and they won't battle the way we would.

Day Two – Worcestershire 199 (Botham 73, Watkinson 7/69), Lancashire 126/2 (Mendis 70). Lancashire need 140 to win.

 HICK:

Beefy played exceptionally well, considering the state of the game and that he was worried about a death threat. We had the Special Branch in the dressing room and they kept close to him throughout this trip. Apparently they're taking the threats seriously because in their message to the police they used a code that appeared when someone was actually murdered in Manchester. So when Beefy went out today he joked that he was going to enjoy it because it might be his last innings. I suppose that's the best way to approach such a thing. When it was our turn to field we joked about having a lottery to see who was going to stand either side of him at first and third slip! I think our leg-pulling helped get Beefy through all this. He certainly batted in the old manner. One six he hit off Paul Allott went miles over the boundary after he'd given him the charge. When he plays like that, pressure falls off his partner – you just have to work the ones and twos and give him his head. He's at his best, coming in behind the batters who've laid down a good foundation and then he can murder tired bowlers. When he hits so straight, there's a very real danger of getting smacked on the body as you back up. I found a novel way to get out. As Mike Watkinson ran in to me, I had a premonition that he was going to bowl it short, and he did – outside the off-stump. I was a little slow on the shot and I had a late stab at it, to be caught by third man. I felt a fool.

When they batted again, the wicket seemed to have eased a little and Mendis played very well. He had a bit of luck, nicking a few over the slips, but I'd happily do the same if it guaranteed me 70 every innings. I caught him eventually at slip, leaning over to my right as he chopped at one, but he has given Lancashire a real chance of beating us. Mike Atherton looks well set and I've given him two escapes, dropping one low to my left and then leaning forward. Both at slip. I hope I haven't lost us the game.

Judging by Beefy's attitude tonight, we're home and dry. We went to a cricket forum at Middleton, organised by Dave Roberts, who knows a lot of clubs around here, and it was a fun evening. Beefy, Dill and myself sat on the forum to answer questions but they'd only come to hear if Beefy had any outrageous thoughts. He kept saying, 'When we've beaten you lot tomorrow,' and although some tried to take him on and ask the questions they wouldn't dare ask face to face, he wasn't bothered. He doesn't care whether they believe what he says or not, it's all a laugh to him. I hope he's right about tomorrow's result.

DILLEY:

It was a brave knock from Beefy, considering the death threats and that it was only a few weeks ago that he had his cheekbone broken. On their side, only Mendis and Atherton have shown the same guts. Mendo was very impressive. I'd take him to the West Indies as an expendable opener: he's too old for the future but good enough to do you a stop-gap job out there. When I hit him a couple of times on the helmet, they looked nasty blows, but he battled through. I didn't see why I should slacken off, because I owed it to my team-mates to keep up the hostility. Although they have plenty of wickets in hand and don't need too many runs I still think we'll do them. All we need is to separate Atherton and Fairbrother early on, because from the evidence of the first innings the rest of them won't fancy it if we keep pitching it short and aiming for the throat area.

The cricket forum tonight was good fun, although I had to be at my most diplomatic when they fired questions at me about South Africa. I had to take refuge in the old platitudes about

'You've got to go out there and see it at first hand before you can comment.' The main entertainment of course came from Beefy – Hicky and I were just there to see how many would try to take the piss out of him. Graeme handles these public occasions very impressively for a twenty-three-year-old. He suffers Joe Public so much better than the rest of us – he is very affable, ideal media material.

Day Three – Lancashire 229 all out (Atherton 59, Dilley 5/94). Worcestershire won by 36 runs.

 HICK:

Dill bowled fast and straight again this morning and no one – apart from Atherton – lasted very long. I was impressed by Atherton. He used the pace of the pitch to guide his strokes to the boundary, he looked composed and solid. But when Fairbrother went, top-edging a hook, one end was open. Jesty never looked comfortable and nicked one to me off the shoulder of the bat, while Watkinson had a dreadful time against Dill. He was hit all over the place, kept battling on, but then I caught him. Behind the wicket we felt there was a chance of a catch every ball because Dill was bowling so straight and Beefy was also swinging it away from the bat. Some might say that Dill's bowling constituted intimidation but what was he to do on a wicket like that? Batsmen get more chances to play on flat wickets than a quickie gets a suitable surface, so was he still supposed to pitch it up so he could be driven? I think intimidation is when a batsman is ducking four or five balls an over but not if the ball is chest high and he can leave it alone. I took five catches in the slips in this innings and none of them were off the glove – they were all off the edge as the batsmen played forward, beaten for pace. No intimidation there.

We owed Lancashire this defeat after May but there were no complaints from them. There should be more pitches in county cricket like this one at Old Trafford. Once I got used to the pace of the pitch, I'd love to bat on it. Their groundsman certainly seems to know his trade because in the last few years I've played there on a square turner, a good batting wicket and now this one, an absolute flier. It certainly made for an exciting match and we're delighted to open up a gap between ourselves and Lancashire.

DILLEY:

I was pleased with my stamina, that I lasted for two hours, bowling fast in sultry conditions. Could this be an omen for me for next week's Test at Old Trafford? I hope that the wicket for the Test is like this one because the Aussies won't fancy the ball flying around their ears. A quick, bouncy pitch would negate Alderman's lbws because the ball would be going over the top of the stumps. Lawson isn't quick any more and although Merv Hughes will get bounce, he's not that dangerous. If we can be sure of a fast pitch, we should pick someone like Devon Malcolm or Greg Thomas to give them the hurry-up. It could just be the turning point in the series.

I thought the vital wicket came when Graeme caught Atherton at slip off Beefy. You should always look at wickets in the context of the particular match and Atherton's was a good deal more vital than getting four tail-enders. He looks a good, sound batsman, the type who'll do well eventually in the West Indies. At the moment he deserves the chance of making runs on flat wickets against India, Sri Lanka and New Zealand, rather than getting demolished in the Caribbean in a few months' time. Then they'd only tell him to go back and learn his trade in county cricket, and leave him there.

So we've won an important game and it will do wonders for our confidence. I think I've been more optimistic about the rest of the season than some of the lads – partly I suppose because, if you admit there's no chance, there really *is* no chance and also because I've seen too much defeatism already this year in the England dressing room. We needed to perform well at Old Trafford and we also showed a lot of physical courage. The mood is good as we travel down endless motorways by coach to Hove. We have coffee-making facilities on board, a toilet and a dustbin full of wine and cold beers. There's a great party atmosphere, the lull before the storm of another game tomorrow against Sussex. I sleep off the exertions during the seven-hour journey, waking up to chuckle at Steve O'Shaughnessy's latest own-goal. Steve is packing up the county game this season, but we thought he should come up to Old Trafford with us, as social secretary and a former Lancashire player. Now we all know he never really got on with Cyril Washbrook, their president. When we were having lunch today, Washbrook said, 'Well played' to Steve, who then turned round and said, 'Do you know summat, that's the first three words he's spoken to me for years.' Classic O'Shaughnessy – we'll miss him.

To Hove, then, and two games Worcestershire would be expected to win. Sussex, in a transitional phase, were fourth from the bottom of the championship, while Worcestershire were now second to Essex, 167 points to 203 with the same number of games played. Essex had just rolled over Kent inside two days at Southend, so Worcestershire's satisfaction at beating Lancashire was tinged with disappointment that they had not stolen a march on the leaders. Worse was to come for Worcestershire. They lost by four wickets off the last ball in the championship game, then on the Sunday Sussex beat them by 14 runs.

⊖ HICK:

The stay at Hove began badly when we were moved out of the hotel because one or two didn't like their rooms. After a long trip down from Manchester we could've done without moving round the corner after dumping our suitcases in the bedrooms. It did seem a bit silly, when you consider how little time we spend in our rooms. Things never seemed to go right after that. On the first morning Gordon Lord broke his right knee-cap, pushing forward to the medium-pacer Tony Dodemaide. That just about sums up Gordon's season. He battled away bravely up at Old Trafford against quick bowling and now he gets toppled by a fluke injury, wearing new pads, by a medium-pacer. We all had a bad day on Saturday, apart from Tim Curtis, who made another valuable hundred. I got nought and a bad nought it was too. I was very close to lbw on the back foot as soon as I went in, then I forced Dodemaide to gully where David Smith, a former team-mate at Worcester, caught it with a big smile on his face. My only consolation was that I could watch a lot of the Open golf on the TV and read the papers. I seem to have read more newspapers in the dressing room this season than ever before. On the pitch, Martin Weston cracked 70, playing naturally, while Beefy got bowled by a young off-spinner called Brad Donelan. It was very funny – Beefy had watched him toss the ball up and said in the dressing room, 'It's either him or me.' So we settled down to watch the fun. He smashed a couple of fours then got bowled, trying to cut one that was too far up. We ended the day on 278 for 7 and that's no kind of platform for victory on a good batting pitch. I don't know if we were experiencing any reaction from Old Trafford, but I certainly felt sluggish when I went out to bat.

On Sunday we never got going and we lost an important game we would've expected to win. We didn't bowl well and the fact that I had to bowl at the death proves we weren't at our best because you'd normally be relying on Radford or Botham then. Our batters got themselves in, then out, including me (for 35) – another thin edge to the keeper after another attempt to run the ball down to third man! Afterwards Phil Neale asked us what we were thinking of and said that we could say goodbye to the Refuge for this season – that only made the championship game here even more important. But Monday was another frustrating day, with Sussex all out near the end for 301, just 19 runs short of us. That meant a lot of jockeying and wheeler-dealing on the last day if we were to force victory on such a good wicket.

The only Worcestershire player to emerge with credit was Ian Botham. He bowled magnificently in the heat, bowling forty overs and taking the first seven wickets. He hit a great line and kept swinging it. The way he trapped Ian Gould lbw was very impressive. He'd been bowling it across the left-hander but then bent one in on him as he played no stroke. Gould was on his way before the umpire put his finger up. David Smith was given out lbw and stalked off waving his bat, saying he'd nicked it, but he had been out earlier and hadn't gone. He nicked one down the leg-side and

Steve Rhodes took a diving catch. Steve said he noticed a big deflection off the bat and Beefy's appeal was a formality. By his immediate reaction we knew that Smithy knew he'd hit it, but he stayed where he was. Somehow Beefy kept going and the fall of wickets obviously helped. If Neal Radford had ventured out on to the field, he wouldn't have bowled so many overs but after smashing 66 not out in the morning, Radders complained of migraine and seemed quite happy to disappear into the darkness. That left Dill, who bowled badly and was troubled by his knee again, and Beefy with a new ball. I nipped in to take three late wickets to deny Beefy all ten. He deserved all ten for his great heart.

In the end we lost the game off the last ball, but we were never in with a chance of victory in the last hour. We had to give them a generous declaration to tempt them and 250 off 51 overs was fair enough. They bowled properly in the morning and I played well for my 110. Early on, I had a torrid time – almost caught at bat/pad before I'd scored – and two balls later a big appeal for lbw. I still haven't got a pair! Then I started telling myself, 'Get forward,' and, after a square drive for four, felt much better. I hit Donelan over the top for six and I was away. I reached my thousand runs for the season (two months later than last year) and although this was only my fourth hundred I feel I'm coming through now. I want to end up with an average of more than 50 and there's no reason why I can't get four or five more hundreds before the season ends. When they batted, we were again short of Dill and Radford, who only bowled six overs for some reason. Again Beefy was tremendous, bowling throughout the innings and sending down just one bad over. Phil Neale dangled the carrot with my off-spin, but they paced it well. We should've prevented the win, though, if Radford had been awake. Off the last ball of the game, Pigott hit me up in the air at mid-wicket, ten yards to Radford's right. He left it to Dolly, forty yards away on the lap, then at the last minute went for the catch. He not only allowed the ball to bounce before going for it, but then fumbled it as they completed the second run to win. I was furious, had a go at him there and then. We knew we couldn't win but professional pride didn't allow us to hand it to them on a plate. He didn't want to accept responsibility for appearing to dip out of an easy catch. Perhaps Radders is having a few problems at the moment.

So we've lost. It was a long journey home on the coach and we got back about eleven o'clock. We have to be on the ground tomorrow morning for another championship match. It gets mentally tiring as well as the physical strain of getting up, getting out and doing it again. We've got another three weeks of this before we get time off, three weeks in which the title could be decided.

DILLEY:

I firmly believe we lost these two important games because of the travel arrangements. We were shattered when we got down to Hove and the performance of changing hotels when we got there wasn't the best preparation. It was a diabolical journey down – everybody seems to be on holiday and the old motorway cones were much in evidence. I remember how much I used to enjoy all this when I first started with Kent. What could be more fun than going to different parts of the country, staying in nice hotels, trying out the local real ale? I thought Barry Richards was mad to go on about the boredom of county cricket but now, when it comes to travel, I can see his point.

Anyway, on the first day at Hove it was clear that the batters wanted to stand at slip all day, while the bowlers didn't fancy anything but watching the Open golf on TV and applauding the efforts of our batsmen out in the middle. By Saturday night we were going nowhere and we were obviously jaded, needing to sparkle on Monday. My knee has flared up again after the Lancashire game and I spent the Sunday in the hotel with an ice-pack on it. It was bound to swell up with prolonged bowling and it's now a case of trying to control the swelling and getting me through selected games. I can't see any chance of me playing in the Old Trafford Test on Thursday. So I listened to the progress of the lads on *Cricketcall* and reflected that, with four games to go, we have no chance of overhauling Lancashire and Essex after this latest defeat. I managed to win the team sweep when Mark Calcavecchia beat Greg Norman in a sudden-death play-off. Pity Norman went into that bunker – I like the way he approaches the game.

Beefy's effort on Monday was typical. He actually enjoyed the situation of not having to give up the ball and proving he could still get men out. They can say what they like about him, but he has a big heart. I honestly thought he'd seize up when he came off at the end, but he could still summon up the will to stagger up the steps to Tony Pigott's squash-club bar. People are still scared of getting out to him. They don't want to be done by bad balls and so they bat differently against him than they would against anyone else. It seems so obvious these days what he's trying to do with the ball because he has to change his action noticeably for a particular delivery. He has to get his shoulder round for an out-swinger to the right-hander and he's so much more open now when he's spearing it into the batsman. Yet people keep falling for it – a lot must be due to sheer force of personality. Just as well he still believes in himself because I bowled crap, absolute rubbish with no rhythm or control. Paul Parker again got after me – there seems no point in ever bowling at him because he always hammers me around the park. The knee troubled me and I felt guilty about limping off with my cartilage falling apart when poor old Radford was already off with a splitting headache after his major innings in the morning.

We had a tall order on this final day. We had to score quick runs and then bowl them out. We managed the first objective with Hicky playing really well against good, testing bowling but we lacked the bowlers to complete the second task. Another great effort from Beefy to bowl unchanged and I felt really sorry for him at the death when he was hit for eighteen in one over. That more or less decided it, although they still wouldn't have won if Radders had taken that catch off Hicky. Everybody shouted, 'Yours, Radders!' but he didn't make it. I didn't know migraine affected your hearing.

There was *some* consoling news for Worcestershire as they travelled home. Essex had become the first county to be docked twenty-five points for preparing a substandard pitch. In the last two matches at Southend, the Kent game had finished inside two days while the Yorkshire one was a hazardous affair for batsmen. The revised county table now meant that Essex had a lead of twenty-seven points over Worcestershire rather than fifty-two. It was the first time in cricket history that a club had been punished so severely. There was no right of appeal. The TCCB had ruled that although the Yorkshire game was not held at the county's headquarters at Chelmsford, Essex were still responsible for conditions at out-grounds like Southend.

DILLEY:

You've got to feel sorry for them because they'd had problems getting their groundsmen to work on what is an out-ground, but it's not as if the law has just been sprung on Essex. Perhaps they should've called in Harry Brind before the match, as we did two months ago. It wouldn't have helped their case that the pitch for the Kent game was reported to Lord's. It'll be difficult for Essex to recover from this – they'll start to think the world is against them. They can whinge as much as they like but it might mean we'll be playing at Lord's next April as the county champions. Lots of other grounds have been iffy and at the start of the season I'd have said the first club to cop it would either be Nottinghamshire, Derbyshire or us – certainly not Essex. But we didn't have dubious pitches intentionally and I'm sure that's the same with Essex, because we are both good sides and don't need an unfair advantage. Essex are unlucky – but the rules were there.

HICK:

I've got no sympathy for Essex. You play to the rules laid down at the start of the season. Perhaps they went for Essex because they're so far ahead at the top of the table that a loss of twenty-five points might not be so crucial, but we shall see. You must be able to control your home pitches. Something must be done to improve county wickets because they're not doing English cricket any good at all. At least we're trying at Worcester, with Harry Brind's co-operation. Essex have got used to winning in the 1980s and they tend to want things all their own way. When you play against them, they moan when lbw appeals are turned down that weren't even worth making and they make a point of whingeing loudly. Now we want to beat them at Colchester in a fortnight and go on to win the championship by at least twenty-six points. That way no one can complain about the twenty-five points' deduction.

The vagaries of the New Road pitches can be gauged by the first-class statistics so far of Hick's batting. Overall he averaged 47, but at home it was 16 while away it was 73. While Hick and his team-mates started a championship game at New Road against Surrey, Dilley travelled up to Manchester on the eve of the Test, convinced he was wasting his time.

◁▭▭ DILLEY:

I told Micky Stewart I had no chance of playing and the England physio Laurie Brown and I went off to see a surgeon. He told me that the cartilage had been nicked again and that another look inside was due. It's depressing to face yet another knee operation but I can handle things that lead to positive results, that mean I can play again. It's now a case of getting through the rest of the season without having the op. Worcestershire will be rationing my appearances from now on, so I'll have to pick up wickets in my specific games. At least I won't have to rush around on Sundays, so I can stay fresh for the important stuff on Monday mornings.

As for the Test wicket, I had a word with the groundsman and he told me it would be nothing like the one we had for the county game last week. He was clearly under orders. So we go into a Test two-down on a slow, low pitch. Crazy. It's not even going to be a raging turner. How do they expect us to turn the series around?

I watched the first two days at Old Trafford before I headed home for more treatment, and it was another depressing experience as we were bowled out cheaply and they batted us right out of the game. My feeling is one of disbelief that we're playing so badly and that they're on such a good roll. Poor Graham Gooch keeps getting out lbw and yet he's such a great believer in net practice that there must be a fluke about it. He's desperate to do well and such a good player that I can't believe Alderman has discovered a flaw in Graham's technique so late in his career. I enjoyed Robin Smith's hundred. He will slaughter every Test attack other than the West Indies and even against them he'll give a good account of himself. I thought Merv Hughes got away with murder against Robin, giving so much verbal abuse. If an England player had behaved like that, it would've been a hefty fine for dissent or loutish behaviour, but because it's Merv it's okay because he's a character, a bit of a laugh. He wasn't that much of a character when we played against him in Australia a couple of years ago. The ball kept disappearing over the boundary off his bowling and he didn't have much time for his antics. Beefy's nought when he missed a swipe at Trevor Hohns was typical. I was watching it on TV in the dressing room and thought, 'Bloody hell, he's going down the wicket to him. But he's just come in. Oh no, he's missed it.' If he'd been in good batting form, the ball would've disappeared: remember what he did to Craig McDermott as soon as he came in during the Edgbaston Test of '85? One of his strengths is that he plays to character and he'd be wrong to change. It might have been a good idea to hang around a little before launching himself at the leg-spinner, but that's the way he plays. He's definitely worried about the death threats, even though he tries not to show it. But the Special Branch are in the dressing room all the time and he's edgy. It can't be easy to walk out on to the field, setting yourself up as a target for some crackpot with a rifle.

By the time I left Old Trafford, there was a fatalistic atmosphere. Everyone's after David Gower's head. I feel sorry for the guys involved – they're mates of mine and if we are going to lose I just wish we could put up a better performance than we've managed so far this summer. It's a huge mystery that we've played so badly and they've looked so good. Some of the members in the Old Trafford pavilion are very free with their snide remarks if we play badly. They were made to look pretty stupid in the one-day international there against New Zealand in '86. They booed us off the park when we'd been smashed around but a few hours later, thanks to Bill Athey and Goochy, we'd won a high-scoring game.

Then we were the greatest. Just shows how fickle some supporters can be. At the moment they're having a ball at David Gower's expense.

As Dilley returned home for a momentous weekend, Worcestershire were wrapping up an encouraging win over Surrey. Set 388 to win 109 overs, Surrey lingered but were dismissed with 8.4 overs left for 285. With Essex drawing against Middlesex, that narrowed the gap between them to just eleven points. Worcestershire's first-innings total of 284 was the best by any side at New Road this season.

⊖ HICK:

It was the first pitch we've felt happy about here this season. It looked slightly under-prepared but it turned out low and slow. We played good cricket to win by sheer perseverance. It was bound to be a game of patience on such a slow pitch and, with so many young players in the side, we did very well to win. Any team lacking Dilley, Botham, Curtis and Newport would feel it, but McEwan kept bouncing in to take wickets and Radford took eight wickets in the match on a wicket that suited his skidding trajectory. Once again our tail showed resilience. We got from 111 for 7 to 284 all out, with Steve Rhodes getting a priceless 83. Early on in his Worcester career, Steve couldn't drive through the off-side very well and he kept asking me how to do it. I'd just smile and say, 'You'll learn', and now he has shots all round the wicket. Richard Illingworth also enjoyed himself, chiselling out 70. He has one particular shot he just loves to play. He'll put his foot straight down the wicket and half-crouching he'll flat-bat it past point. Then he'll stand there with his bat above his head, savouring the moment. Given the chance he'll play the shot against any bowler, fast or slow.

On the second evening we crashed on in search of a declaration and I played well. In the first innings I'd been trapped lbw for 9, playing back to a ball that kept low, but next day I felt very confident. I really should've got a hundred, but with the declaration due I played across the line to the spinner Keith Medlycott and was lbw for 85. I was pretty disgusted with myself at the shot and when we went out to field Chris Balderstone, one of the umpires, gave me an old-fashioned look. It was the first time I'd played across the line and I would've got a hundred if I'd played properly, but it's a team game and I couldn't hang around.

Surrey crumbled on the last day when it looked as if they were going to save it easily. They're now in the same position as we were a couple of years back – with promising young players and a tendency to collapse when pressure is put on them. But credit to us. Apart from our earlier absentees we got through the final day without Martin Weston (broken finger) and Paul Bent (stomach upset). So McEwan and Radford had to bowl a lot of overs. They bowled to their field and never gave up on the batters. They just wore them down in the end.

The day got even better this evening when Mum called me from home to say that the baby had just arrived, safe and well – and my sister's fine too! She said young Bradley looked just like me, which means it's off to a good start. I finally managed to track down my brother-in-law as he was celebrating in a restaurant with all his mates. We chatted for twenty minutes and I suddenly saw a different side to him – he seemed all soft and gooey about the experience. I wish I was there now to join in the celebrations. We had a few drinks tonight and Jackie said, 'You'd better get a hundred tomorrow now, for Bradley.' I'll be trying.

Hick was as good as his word. He made 147 and helped Paul Bent add 135 for the second wicket as Bent made his maiden first-class hundred. A total of 402 for 6 declared was insurance against defeat, further evidence of Harry Brind's skill, and placed Kent on the wrong end of a ten-wicket defeat. With a seven-wicket win on Sunday, it seemed that Worcestershire were slipping into a higher gear just at the right time.

 HICK:

I wanted a big hundred when I went in to bat. There was no danger in the wicket, although it was a little slow. You just needed to discipline yourself in your stroke selection. I was surprised at a couple of my sixes, though – playing inside out to the left-arm spinner Davis and hitting him over extra cover. I don't usually play that shot, so I must've felt confident. Certainly my footwork was better and my driving worked well. Paul Bent played very positively, but I was surprised that he seemed quite happy to be out once he'd passed his hundred. We still had another couple of hours' batting ahead of us and I had my eyes on a double hundred – 'fill your boots' time after this season's problems – but he kept playing shots and eventually chased a wide one on 144. I got myself out in an annoying way – chopping one on from a ball of full length just outside the off-stump. I was out exactly the same way next day in the Sunday game. Kent didn't look terribly interested on Sunday and they were troubled by stomach upsets on Monday, so they weren't exactly stern resistance. It must be hard for them this summer after doing so well last year. They're bottom of the championship table and second bottom in the Sunday league, so August could be a long month for them. Once we got them to follow on, the game was ours, even though the weather turned a little dodgy, with the light too dark for the quicker bowlers at times. Just as in the Surrey game, we stuck at it and chipped away at them. Stuey Lampitt took five wickets and looked a very good prospect. He hit the seam, bowled on one side of the wicket, got close to the stumps and picked up a few lbws by bowling straight. He's someone to watch. He's been in the wings for a year or two, putting up fine all-round performances in the Birmingham League and the second team, and he has a good, mature head on his shoulders. As a batsman he's very underrated and although at the moment he won't get in ahead of Rhodes, Newport or Illingworth, he's got it in him to bat higher up.

So we're in good heart for Lancashire tomorrow in the NatWest. The captain said to me today, 'I don't think we need to motivate you for this one,' and he's right. They caught us at a bad time in May and we want to get to Lord's again for the final. If we beat Lancashire, I'm sure we'll get there.

While Dilley's old county spent a fraught weekend at Worcester, he was getting ready for the South African storm to break.

═► DILLEY:

Sunday, 30 July. David Graveney phoned me to say that the news was going to break over the next forty-eight hours. In a sense I'm relieved, although it would've been better to have it overshadowed by the soccer season in a few weeks' time, but that's just being selfish. It's been a strain keeping it secret while trying to give of my best on the field. Every day it's been in my mind at some stage. So now Old Trafford marks the last time I shall be part of the England set-up. A rather anti-climactic way to go. At David Graveney's request, I sent back my non-availability form to Lord's, confirming I wouldn't be going on any of this winter's England tours. It was designed to arrive on Tuesday morning, when we expected the story to be out. I can't believe how slapdash the TCCB have been about not asking us more about our intentions. Why didn't Ted Dexter and Micky Stewart ask us specific questions in the last two months? By the end of May, most of us knew we were going to South Africa yet the TCCB didn't get round to the availability list deadline till the end of July. It's almost as if they wanted to give us breathing space. Between the Lord's Test and now, I've had no approach from the TCCB asking what my plans are for the winter. I'd have wanted to know what was going on if I were them, and then I could've made the decision on whether to keep the South Africa-bound players in the Ashes series. Yet I honestly don't believe the atmosphere in the England dressing room was affected by this business. As professionals you know what you have to do and we were very disappointed we couldn't do the specific jobs expected of us. I didn't perform badly because I was thinking about South Africa, although I admit I've been a little down about having to keep it all secret.

Monday, 31 July. The offers to talk about South Africa are going up and up. Now it's £20,000 from the tabloid newspaper that offered me £10,000 during the Edgbaston Test. No chance. I shall fulfil my part of the contract. I see Matthew Maynard has admitted to the papers that he's considering a great offer from South Africa. It would've been better if he'd kept quiet, because the quicker it all comes out, the more flak we're going to get. David Graveney says a statement will be issued on behalf of every player and that if we have any sense we should just use that. I rang our club chairman Duncan Fearnley to tell him what I was doing and he simply said, 'Okay, fine – thanks for telling me, and good luck.' I was worried how Basil D'Oliveira might react but when we talked about the possibility of a tour last year he said, 'You're only in this game for a short time. If you can make money, then make it.' So he should be all right. There's no question of last-minute second thoughts. Call it mercenary if you like, but I don't play this game for the same reasons I used to. I play cricket because it's the thing I do best and it's not going to last much longer for me. If they turned round now and said no company in the world can trade with South Africa, it would make a difference to my going. But companies are allowed to trade, so why can't I go there and play sport?

Tuesday, 1 August. The papers have had a dart at the names of the players this morning, but the official news didn't break till eleven o'clock, just as the last day of the Test was starting. I saw our names come up on the TV screen and my initial reaction was relief. Most of those in the party have already been to South Africa, while bowlers like me and Neil Foster have weighed up our injuries against this lucrative offer. I was a little surprised not to see Graham Gooch among the names, bearing in mind his past involvement, and also to see Mike Gatting in the squad. Clearly he was a late entry, because I wasn't aware he was a runner. That gives us more credibility because under Gatt we'll be going all out to win. The way England's summer was going, there was a chance that Gatt might have been reinstated as captain, especially as he and Micky Stewart get on so well, but he was bitter at the way he'd been treated by the TCCB in the past year. Bowlers like Paul Jarvis and Phil DeFreitas had signed up, partly through frustration. One bad game for England and they're out, whereas the batters get more chances. I'm surprised that Matthew Maynard's with us because he's so young, but he hasn't had a sniff of England selection this year and must be feeling disillusioned. He's one of the few who could still play for England in seven years' time, because he'll only be thirty then. Beefy's absence reduces our attractiveness. I know he was sorely tempted, but he earns too much money from outside sources to be able to afford to go to South Africa, even though he'd be handsomely paid for it.

Of those who have turned down the offer, some of them have moral objections while others want to stay with England, and I respect both sentiments. I'm not saying we're going as ambassadors. I'm not even saying we'll change anything in that country. It's just that cricket has done a hell of a lot of good to integrate people of all races and colours in South Africa. At least on a Saturday or Sunday afternoon they can compete on equal footing. I'll do whatever coaching they want in the townships because that will give me a lot of enjoyment.

Throughout today people have clearly thought about talking to me about South Africa, but thankfully they've respected my privacy. The press haven't said anything to me, probably because they know I'll just refer them to our statement. It's rather amusing to see the possible clashes of personality in our squad. There's me and Chris Cowdrey, for a start. He's here today with Kent and although he knows I left because I disapproved of his replacing Chris Tavaré as captain of Kent, we have played on the same side since. He captained me in the Leeds Test last year and we both put our past differences behind us. It's his problem that he's having to rebuild a Kent side that's lost so many experienced players in the past five years. I wonder how Chris Broad and Tim Robinson will get on. I can't see them spending much time together away from the cricket! David Graveney and Bill Athey are hardly bosom pals after David lost the captaincy to Bill at Gloucestershire last year. But we're professionals, getting very well paid, and I'm sure we can all forget the past while we're out there.

I know that people will knock some of the players in this squad, saying there are a few has-beens in it. But in all modesty I think I can claim that a 1989 England side would contain Emburey, Gatting, Broad, Foster and myself if we were all fit and in form. Anyway, the words of Mike Vockins keep coming back to me tonight: 'Just concentrate on doing your best for Worcestershire now.' I owe them that. Starting tomorrow.

HICK:

I was fairly sure there'd be a rebel side to South Africa this winter – in fact they were all talking about it when I was in Zimbabwe six months ago. I've spent a fair amount of time in South Africa, playing schools tournaments three years on the trot and also taking holidays on the Natal coast. I think it's fair enough that they should go out and play there if they wish. People are still trading with South Africa and cricket is used as a scapegoat. Golfers and tennis players still go there but cricket suffers more than any other sport. You just take the risk if you go – it's a matter for the individual.

THE HOME STRAIGHT

August began with another packed house at New Road and a highly professional performance by Worcestershire, to beat Lancashire by seven wickets in the NatWest Trophy quarter-final. Lancashire could not break free of tight bowling and sharp fielding, and their total of 237 for 9 off sixty overs was never going to be enough against a team intent on revenge for two bad defeats early in May. Graeme Hick chose the occasion to play a majestic innings of 90 not out, winning the game in the grand manner with a six over extra cover off Paul Allott.

HICK:

I haven't felt better at the crease all season than I did today. Right from the start I felt positive. I got off the mark by pushing a four past Jack Simmons at mid-on. I knew there was one to Jack, because he doesn't move that quickly these days and, as soon as I played it, I called 'Yes!', only to see the ball whizz past him. I thought, 'That was well timed,' and it went on in the same way. Immediately before tea I hit Simmons for a straight six and it felt terrific. Just before any interval the spinners always come on to whip through their overs, but I was feeling so positive that I didn't want to be dictated to just because tea was due. Mid-on and mid-off were both back, but I fancied taking them on. My feet just seemed to take me down the wicket and the ball soared over the TV commentary box. If I'd got out, I know I'd have looked a complete fool but it was a big confidence-boost to take into the dressing room at tea. The skipper gave me a dry smile and said, 'Just as well it came off,' but he knew I had a bit of bubble in me today and that I was looking to be there at the end. After tea we managed to get Simmons taken off and that was an important moment because he's always a valuable bowler in these games. After that it was plain sailing until Paul Allott came on to bowl with just a few overs needed. Many in the crowd were shouting to me, 'Hit another six!', but I wasn't looking for one. The first ball outside the off-stump was blocked by me into the covers. The next one was well up and I just played it with a straight bat. I looked up, fully expecting to have to run, but then saw it sail into the crowd for six. I was amazed and delighted that it all seemed to be flowing again. But it wasn't just about me today – it was our best all-round display of the season. No team would've beaten us today, we felt so confident.

━━▶ DILLEY:

Whatever Graeme says about today's innings, it's bound to be modest but I tell you it was a high-class innings against good bowlers. It was a pleasure to be on the same side and watch such talent. Those two sixes were wonderful shots, timed so sweetly – he just seemed to let his arms go and the ball sailed into the far blue yonder. The confidence he showed in hitting Simmons for six in the over before tea was a tremendous help to the lads in the dressing room. With a player like that on your side, you feel as if you've got an extra man. As for me I didn't bowl all that well. Even though I've never been a big wicket-taker in the limited-overs stuff, I was struggling for rhythm after missing a week. But it was a disciplined performance from all our bowlers and it was a good effort from Beefy to take five wickets. A wicket every two and a half overs in your allotted twelve isn't bad going, especially when the slog starts. It was nice to play on a flat wicket at home. That's how it should be in a match of this importance. The public have come to see a lot of runs and a long game, not some medium-pacer getting the ball to spit up off a length.

Friday, 4 August. We've fetched up at Colchester after a diabolical journey lasting more than three hours from St Pierre near Chepstow. The traffic on the M25 was so bad that we pulled off and had a couple of pints waiting for it to ease. The Friday night trek is always a nightmare in summer. You may well wonder why we were at St Pierre: we were playing a benefit golf match for Paul Pridgeon and we attended a dinner there last night. It's a fantastic place to play golf: it's lovely to be on the course where they stage professional tournaments, rather like village cricketers must feel when they play in their own final every year at Lord's, I suppose. Now we can judge just how good the pros are after playing this course.

I've just had my first piece of personal abuse over the South African decision. I was walking out of the hotel this morning when this bloke passed me and, in front of his mates, said, 'Oh, there's that —— traitor.' I ignored him, as any sensible person would. I've had some letters asking me to change my views, expressed in polite terms. One wrote, 'I was there eleven years ago and believe me, it's a dreadful place.' Well, at least he's been there and I respect his views, even if they are a little out of date – many of our critics have never been anywhere near the place to judge for themselves. Mike Gatting said some rather naive things at a press conference the other night, when he said he knew nothing about Apartheid, that he was just a sportsman, and so on. He should have kept quiet because his words will be seized on and a great deal of capital will be made out of it. Much as I like and admire Gatt, he's no diplomat. Paul Jarvis ought to have kept his thoughts to himself as well – all that stuff about having to manage on a £65,000 mortgage doesn't impress many people who can't even afford to buy a house. We mustn't give extra ammunition to those who are going to slag us off anyway. Let them make up their own minds on the issue, instead of us making provocative, ill-judged remarks. Why can't we all just stick to the agreed statement put out last Tuesday? Down my local pub everyone's wished me 'good luck' but I also respect those who disagree with my actions. At least in this country people can make up their own minds, even if it's only from what they read in the papers. As long as they're not abusive to me, I can understand their criticism, even though there are too many dogmatic statements flying around about South Africa.

HICK:

We've played a lot down at St Pierre since Beefy's joined us at Worcester: he seems to know everybody and he fixed up the visits for us. It's a big, challenging course of championship standard and you know that if your drive goes astray, then you'll end up against one of those enormous trees. Our most consistent player is Tim Curtis. He plays off an eight handicap, Beefy off ten and I'm off around twelve. TC is the slowest player I know. He takes an eternity to line up his putts as we snore loudly alongside the green. We call him 'Ken Brown' in recognition of his slow play, but he always walks off with the money. I just play and go, I can't be bothered hanging around. I hit it reasonably well off the tee, but my approach work to the greens definitely needs a bit of work. Golf has now taken over from tennis and hockey as my second sport and I shall work hard when the season's finished to get my handicap down. I don't see how it will affect my batting at all – in fact the need to get your shoulder round for the drive is common to both sports.

On the long drive over to Colchester, we talked about the game ahead and the NatWest semi-final draw. I'm delighted we've got Warwickshire at Edgbaston. A sell-out crowd, a local derby and we're the better team nine times out of ten. As for the match tomorrow, we really want to beat Essex. They'll still be thinking about losing twenty-five points instead of us and we'll want to play well against them. We don't need dodgy wickets at home to win the title, in fact that's the last thing we want. The weather is settled and Colchester usually helps the spinners in August. I might be busy with my off-spin! There should be a positive result if the wicket turns. I got 150-odd here a couple of years ago and I'd be happy to repeat that. There's a definite edge to this game.

Day One – Essex 208 (Hicks 5/52, Gooch 51), Worcestershire 113/1.

◯ HICK:

I really enjoyed today. We're in a good position and I took five wickets with my off-spin. It was turning a fair amount and I just tried to bowl a foot outside off-stump and hope for sharp turn. As Phil Neale was tossing up this morning, Geoff Miller walked past and said, 'I hope you're playing your spinner, Phil,' and Phil said, 'I'm playing both.' Geoff said, 'Who's your other spinner then?' This evening Phil said to him, 'Geoff, have you met our other spinner?' He was good fun to bowl at, because as an off-spinner himself he knew what I was trying to do. Now and again, one would go straight on for some reason and Geoff would nod 'Well bowled'. I'd no idea how I was doing it any more than when I used the same grip and it's left the bat like a leg-cutter. I work on the assumption that, if I don't know what's going on, what chance has the batsman? I was a little lucky with some of my wickets. Nasser Hussain came in, played a lot of shots right away, then hit one straight back at me. I went round the wicket to Miller because the ball was turning so much and soon after I'd posted a fielder just behind square leg, he tried to play the ball in that direction too carefully and it went to bat/pad off the edge. Just before lunch, Mike Garnham tried to cut one that wasn't very wide and it hit his off-stump. Phil Neale took a good low catch at squarish mid-wicket to get Derek Pringle, and Tim Curtis caught an even better one at long-on to get Neil Foster. Towards the end I got a little tired and lost concentration, and I expect I'll be even more tired come Tuesday because Richard Illingworth and me are bound to do most of the bowling on this pitch. I reckon Illy will clean up ahead of me, though. I enjoy bowling off-spin. Basil says I've got a good, high action and I suppose my height helps me get bounce. It helps if you're a batter – you understand the little twitching signs and can work out what they're thinking.

We were pretty confident tonight as we tucked into a meal in a lovely country pub a few miles out of Colchester. We'd made a good start in our innings and we thought a lead of around 150 would be more than enough. The Essex boys seemed a little subdued tonight in the bar!

DILLEY:

When Graham Gooch was in, I thought they'd get a good score because, although he was laboured, he's such a good accumulator that he can get a hundred while out of nick. But he chased a wide one off Beefy – well bowled, Golden Arm! – and the rest of them didn't shape too impressively. I was very surprised at the way Nasser Hussain played. I'd heard he played shots, but he was going for everything. He looked as if he'd had no experience at all of playing on a turning wicket, going back to cut the off-spinner and taking it on the glove. He needs to be more selective in his strokeplay, otherwise he'll be sorted out by good bowlers. I was very pleased for Graeme, because I've rated his off-spin for a long time. He has a classic, high action and he turns it a long way. He's going to be an important man in this game, and not just because we need a big innings from him. At lunchtime today, the umpires were considering reporting this wicket to Lord's because it was turning so much. It should be a fascinating game of cricket. Good to see the spinners calling the tune for once, instead of the seamers. There should be more games like this.

Next day, Worcestershire beat Essex by six wickets in the Refuge League and it was an easy victory. Essex, at one stage 108 for 7, were only rescued by some sensible hitting by Neil Foster and Derek Pringle to haul them up to 193 for 9 in their forty overs. Hick (54) and D'Oliveira (60 not out) ensured a comfortable win.

HICK:

We'd used up all our losses for the season on Sundays, so now we wanted to get into the first four to qualify for the semi-finals of the Refuge Cup. So this was a good effort against the side going for the title. Neil Foster's an underrated batsman – he plays straight and drives well – so I hope he's saved his best display for today, rather than in the championship game. I played quite well for my runs, having to work hard against such a professional outfit. I was caught at backward point on the drive – a little disappointed that I wasn't there at the end with Dolly, but he made sure there were no slip-ups.

DILLEY:

I was never going to play because of the need to rest my knee, but Phil Neale suggested I stay away from the ground because there was supposed to be a demonstration from the anti-Apartheid movement against me and Neil Foster. I listened to the game on *Cricketcall* and it sounds a comprehensive win, something of a rarity against Essex. I hope the confidence we've gained today helps us tomorrow when the serious stuff restarts.

Day Two – Worcestershire 447/9 dec. (Curtis 156, Hick 72, Bent 55, D'Oliveira 55), Essex 21/2 in their second innings, still 218 behind.

HICK:

We're pleased with our progress so far. Not only have we established a big first innings lead but we've got Graham Gooch out again, so he's finished in the game. I'm glad to say I got him towards the end of the day. The ball was still quite new and I was a little apprehensive because Gooch can destroy any bowler, but he'd obviously decided to play for the close. The ball pitched a couple of feet outside the off-stump, he got halfway across and then he stabbed at the line of the ball. It crept through bat and pad and hit the top of the off-stump. Perhaps he was worried about playing too positively at the ball because we had a bat/pad at the off-side, but it was a great scalp. Steve Rhodes ran down the wicket and said, 'It drifted away beautifully,' but I think he was a little over-excited. I've no idea how it happened and I'm not bothered!

That made up for a slightly disappointing end to our innings. Although we got a big total, we should've got there earlier, to give us more time to bowl out Essex. The first four wickets put on 336 and then we threw away some of our advantage by getting out when well set and putting pressure on the later batters to score quickly. I got most of my runs in boundaries and, although Foster and John Childs didn't bowl very well, I was pleased at the way I hit the bad balls. Foster was there for the taking when he got me out – he looked despondent, just bowling with his arm, not his body, off a short run, and then I played too soon at a straight drive and he caught me off his own bowling. Tim Curtis again did the sheet-anchor role perfectly, even though he criticised himself for

147

taking a long time over it. That was nonsense – he was doing exactly the right job for the side. Hopefully none of that will matter tomorrow night.

DILLEY:

TC played just the right innings for us today because we needed a big total to bat them out of the game and get them tired and down. Even Essex can get down. Perhaps we relaxed a little after such a good start – we ought to have really hammered them. That was a great piece of bowling by Graeme to get Goochy out because he's the one who can bat all day. He did him 'through the gate' in one of the best pieces of bowling I've seen from an off-spinner. We're really chuffed tonight because Goochy's out. It's rare to bowl out a side like Essex for next to nothing twice in a game, but the ball is turning a hell of a lot now and I don't think they can last out tomorrow. Fatigue is going to be our main problem. We've played a lot of cricket lately.

Day Three – Essex 323/9 (Foster 50 not out, Hick 5/131 off fifty-five overs, Illingworth 4/115 off fifty-two overs. Match drawn.

HICK:

We only have ourselves to blame for not winning. We dropped a catch or two and the spinners got tired. What really cost us the game came when Fozzie swept me to Illingworth at square leg. It wasn't a hard chance, but Illy missed it, ending up sprawling on the ground. Fozzie hadn't been in long and we would've won if that had been taken. I felt sorry for Illy – he was a bit down because he knew he was expected to be the main danger, due to his greater experience and because as a left-hander he'd be turning the ball away from the bat. But he kept beating the bat by a long way and got frustrated. I lost concentration towards the end – my mind was going at a hundred miles an hour and I didn't relax enough and let the conditions do the work. A lack of experience, I suppose. I'm not used to bowling all those overs. My finger is now very sore, with a few cuts and a blood blister on the middle knuckle from gripping the ball so tightly. It was a Reader ball as well and its sharp seam has drawn blood. I'm very stiff and we're all disappointed. They were absolutely delighted at the end, particularly Neil Foster, who played very well indeed. Clearly this game was very important to them. It could've been worse – we might have outplayed them for two and a half days and lost on the final afternoon in a run chase. But it was a very good game of cricket, a refreshing change from ones dominated by seam bowlers and green pitches.

We're now in Weston-super-Mare, after another little three-hour drive. I'm dog-tired, so I slap on a few tapes to keep me concentrating – Dire Straits, Sting, Bryan Adams, good melodic stuff with good words to soothe the nerves. A walk down the seafront at Weston with Dolly for a burger and then bed. Somerset tomorrow: should be a flat wicket. All we need is for Jimmy Cook to take root and we'll struggle to win. We need one after the disappointment at Colchester.

DILLEY:

You have to give credit to Essex for the way they hung on. That was a professional performance from a side full of pride and self-respect. It was good to see so many of us go straight up to Illy and sympathise with him over that dropped catch. We all know how many overs he'd bowled, how tired and stiff he felt and that he was annoyed at not running through them, no matter how hard he tried. In another side, there would've been a deathly hush when that catch went down. A successful side is one that pulls together when it's tough. We can take a lot of encouragement from this game. We have totally outplayed our nearest rivals and they survived by one wicket and about half an hour. I expected Essex to be confident over the last four days but one by one their cards seem to be blowing away. I don't think they've got it in them to last the pace against us now – they give the impression that the world is against them. Of course we talked to them about the twenty-five-points deduction, and we were sympathetic, but we can tell they're down about it. I think we've got them, even though we didn't win here. Our team spirit and harmony are very strong, despite the ridiculous amount of travelling we're doing. It'll be another nine days before we can have a day off.

Day One – Somerset 240 (Roebuck 99, Dilley 3/101), Worcestershire 44/1.

DILLEY:

They got off to a flier, courtesy of yours truly. It was the same story I've had several times this season – nick, smash, nick, play and miss, and I'm going for ten an over. I shouldn't really have been playing but we're down to the bare minimum. No Botham, Radford, Newport, Curtis, Weston, Pridgeon or Lord. Essex might remember that, next time they moan about the twenty-five points. Roebuck surprised me with the dashing strokes he played. I didn't think he had so many. I haven't seen that much of him over the years and now he's been touted around as an England opener. He's also going to Holland next week with an England side as captain, so he must be in the frame for something this winter. Unless he's going to play a part in England's future, there's no point in taking him there as captain. He's a good, organised opener but I just don't know if he can do it at Test level.

I've never played at Weston before, but once you've got used to the poor facilities it's fine. I got used to festival grounds playing with Kent and they do help to remind you of your roots. They've got a good crowd in today and the game is nicely poised. It was a pretty good wicket today, with the odd one misbehaving, but there's no reason why we shouldn't have a good game of cricket.

HICK:

I don't really enjoy playing at Weston. The pavilion is just a wooden shack and the outfield is so rough we couldn't even pat the ball to each other in practice. There was just one net available and nowhere else to have even a throw-down. There's little privacy and some of the autograph-hunters have been very rude today. I never mind signing autographs, even when you're surrounded by about a hundred books being waved in your face, but today one boy just said 'autograph' to me and shoved his book in my direction. I told him to walk back about ten metres, then come up to me and say 'please' and 'thank you' and then I'd sign with pleasure. Manners cost nothing. Perhaps I'm just tired after all that bowling at Colchester.

Roebuck did play well, although Dill was very unlucky. He beat the bat so often, then got smashed for four as soon as he strayed off line. We didn't have a great deal of sympathy for Roebuck getting out on 99 because he's stood his ground once or twice when he's known he edged it. So we don't really get on with him. If he plays that particular way, he's on his own.

Day Two – Worcestershire 302/6 dec. (Hick 72, D'Oliveira 52), Somerset 55/3. Somerset still trail by 7 runs.

━━━► DILLEY:

A very good day. Once he got full batting points, Phil Neale declared because the wicket was helping the seamers more and more. Graeme played superbly but he was done by a near-shooter from Vic Marks. Very sorry for Graeme, because he was sailing to a hundred, but it's not a bad thing to see a ball like that misbehave on the second day when we're building a useful lead – and it wasn't a New Road terror track! Roebuck also copped a shooter this evening and Graeme again nipped in with a useful wicket when he bowled Tavaré. That's two of their best batters out of the way, which just leaves Jimmy Cook. He got 9 in the first innings and I can't believe he's going to fail again. He really is a very, very good player. Graeme Pollock was quite right to forecast he'd get 2000 runs this season, and he raced past that in July. Tav was telling me he's such a refreshing guy to play with. He is very upset if the opposition's leading bowler ever cries off, because he wants to pit his skills against him – he never wants cheap runs. Apparently many of the fast bowlers haven't yet cottoned on to the fact that

Jimmy is a wonderful hooker, so they pitch it halfway down the wicket and the ball keeps disappearing. Jimmy's the man to get out tomorrow if we're going to win.

🌐 HICK:

I was disappointed with the lbw decision against me today. Now I rarely complain about a decision when I'm back in the dressing room. If it's gone against me, I'm usually quiet or say, 'It was a bad enough shot to get me out anyway.' Some batters reckon they're never out, but not me. But today I felt I was particularly unlucky and Dolly, my partner at the time, felt it was going down leg-side. I tried to pull Vic Marks to mid-wicket and it kept low. The umpire's job is easier when it keeps low – it saves thinking about whether it might have bounced over the stumps – but I'm sure it was going down because I wouldn't have played it with a flat bat otherwise. If the ball had been straighter I would've played it to the off-side with a straight bat. I can't believe I misjudged the line that badly. Vic Marks has the reputation of bowling an 'arm ball', so that it swings away towards the slips, but if the umpire thought that a ball pitching on middle and leg from an off-spinner was going to veer away from the bat, that would've been a super leg-cutter – and I don't think Vic bowls those! I found the decision hard to take, because I was batting well after so many bad times this summer and I was working my way towards a hundred. I hope I didn't show my distaste on the field, because I always go promptly when given out, even though I feel it's a bad one. I honestly believe that more often than not an honest batsman knows if it was a good or bad decision.

It had rained overnight and that certainly livened up the wicket. It's now breaking up and a few went through the top when they batted again. Roebuck was amazed when he was bowled by one that kept low – he didn't even seem to want to go for that. I bowled Tavaré when he played it on to the back of his leg and it rolled back on to his stumps. I seem to be getting the knack of nipping in with a good wicket. Jimmy Cook has to be winkled out tomorrow, though. At the start of his innings tonight, he hardly played an attacking stroke, he just waited for the bowlers to stray. He's not too fluent on the off-side – he tends to leave them alone and work straight ones through leg-side. I'd like to see him get a hundred so I could assess just how good a player he is, but please – not tomorrow!

Day Three – Somerset 145 (McEwan 5/28), Worcestershire 87/1. Worcestershire won by nine wickets.

DILLEY:

We had one eye on the weather because we'd been told that gales were on their way, so we didn't want to hang around. In the end it all went to order. Just when they were taking root, Steve McEwan came on and mopped up the tail, like a good opening bowler should. I couldn't manage that and I was very pleased for Macca. He keeps getting the good players out as well. He's coming out of his shell in the past few weeks as he gets more and more confident, and at the moment county cricket must seem a very easy occupation. He and Stuey Lampitt have been a breath of fresh air – they're proud to be playing for their county. We can learn a lot from such enthusiasm; it stops us old pros from being too complacent.

The vital wicket of the day was picked up by Richard Illing-worth. Jimmy Cook had looked in no trouble on a pitch that was crumbling against spin at one end and helping the seamers at the other, but then he played forward and the ball spat up off a length. He took it on the glove and it lobbed up to slip. You can't do anything about those. So it turned out a routine victory when we were expecting a harder fight. Now we just have to keep on winning and getting maximum bonus points as well. The weather might be a problem – it looks as if the long, hot spell may be over – but you can't legislate for that. We mustn't think negatively and complicate things, just keep hanging together and helping each other. Team spirit like ours wins championships.

⊖ HICK:

It was a good wicket to bowl on today. It was cracking up, with a bit of dust flying around, and they were never going to hold out once we got Jimmy Cook. When we went out to get 84 to win, we got a move on because the weather looked a bit threatening. It was nice to get a 'not out' – I haven't had too many of them this season! The not-outs all help when you're hoping to average over 50 in the championship. Pity that Essex won again. I listened to the scores on the carphone on the way to Bournemouth and at one stage it looked as if Northants would get a draw. But we're a lot more confident now than a month ago, and being at the top by fifteen points is a good feeling. If we just keep on winning, we don't have to worry about anyone else. Morale's high – we're playing well with a weakened side and having a good laugh among ourselves. The younger players have all given us a shot in the arm since coming into the side. They've brought their own different brand of humour into the first team and brightened everything up.

So we've fetched up at Bournemouth. We play Hampshire tomorrow. Another few days of living out of suitcases before getting home at last. Another round of dry cleaning: the flannels must be clean every day, one for fielding and one for batting. You've got to look the part on the field. It was nice to get to our hotel early tonight, so we could relax over a beer and put the feet up. I'm a good sleeper when tired and Dolly, my roomie, can kip through anything. I'm always first up at about eight o'clock – I grab the papers, get the ablutions out of the way then shake Dolly awake once I'm out of the shower. He gets another kick five minutes later. At the moment we're both finding it hard to get out of bed.

While the championship race entered its final phase, there were rumours that the rebel tour to South Africa might collapse. This followed the withdrawal from the party of the two black players, Phil DeFreitas and Roland Butcher, who both cited pressure from family and critics as the main reason. There had been a lot of criticism from other black sportsmen about the inclusion of DeFreitas and Butcher in the touring party and both cricketers admitted they had been surprised by the hostility.

 DILLEY:

It was always going to be tougher for Daffy and Butch than for the rest of us. A lot of people have been seeking publicity for themselves over something that two guys have chosen to do of their own free will. I read that some athletes won't even talk to the two black cricketers about their decision, but who the hell are they to think their views would be asked for? What's it got to do with anyone else? I wonder if these so-called amateur athletes would like to talk about the slush funds they get for turning out at various meetings? I'm disappointed they're so narrow-minded and dogmatic. I'm sure there's no danger of the tour falling through. David Graveney's told me that it goes ahead, even if only fourteen players are involved. But I understand there's no shortage of others who want to go, so we'll have sixteen eventually, I imagine.

The team travelled to Bournemouth to play Hampshire.
Saturday 12 August. Day One –
Worcestershire 266/8 (Neale 98).

HICK:

We're happy with that score. The wicket is deteriorating already. It rained here yesterday and the groundstaff didn't have enough cover for the wicket, so there was some flooding on the pitch. The umpires were told the wicket wouldn't last the three days, so it was an important toss to win. You want to bat first when you're told the wicket won't get any better. Phil Neale deserved a hundred – he really worked hard for it. With just a couple of overs left he chopped on an off-break from Chris Smith. He was obviously disappointed but it was more important that he and the lower order gathered some vital runs this evening. Richard Illingworth again battled hard and when he came in at the end, still not out, he had a broad smile on his face. I played well for my 44, until I went for the on-drive. The ball stopped on me and I spooned up a simple catch. Again I felt comfortable at the crease, with the earlier inhibitions gone. I'm looking for a good August now.

DILLEY:

The umpires have reported this pitch already and, with this useful total, that's not the worst news for us. At this stage of the season, we don't want a flat one, with Chris Smith batting hours and hours to get them a draw. They're fourth in the table at the moment, so I assume they're also quite happy about getting a positive result come Tuesday. I was surprised that Malcolm Marshall bowled poorly on a wicket that was helping all the bowlers. Against young openers (Paul Bent and Chris Tolley), he should have pitched it up, cut down on his pace and let the conditions do the work for him, but he bowled too short.

Dilley rested his knee on Sunday, when Worcestershire won an exciting Refuge game by two runs. Chasing 149, Hampshire lost by 2 runs off the last ball.

HICK:

It was a very slow, awkward pitch, a grafter's wicket. I batted for ages to get 30 and then for us it was a case of defending a small total. They had a couple of stands in the middle order but they're missing Robin Smith (he's at the Trent Bridge Test) and they didn't react too well to the pressure. They lost their last seven wickets for 40-odd, and I think that was due to a combination of pressure from us, the bad pitch and their lack of experience in the middle order. Stuey Lampitt bowled at the death, a tall order for a newcomer, but he did very well. He bowled very straight and defended the last over impressively. They needed four off his last ball, but he pitched it up and Tim Tremlett could only hit it out to mid-wicket. All good experience for Stuey – he certainly looks cool under pressure.

Day Two – Worcestershire 325 (Illingworth 71), Hampshire 137 (Lampitt 5/38) and 28/4. Hampshire still 161 behind.

DILLEY:

Stu Lampitt bowled better than I did – he found the right length and hit the seam consistently. It was important to get early break-throughs and almost all of our wickets were in the slips cordon or to the keeper. They were never in it – they seem to have the same sort of subconscious fears about their wicket as we did about ours a month or two back. They appeared to expect to get done by an unplayable one any time. This is a good time to be playing them. With Steve McEwan shooting out the first four tonight – and only one of them a nightwatchman – we're looking to wrap this one up quickly tomorrow.

HICK:

I thought Dill bowled superbly in the first few overs and got us into them early on. He moved it around at a good speed and the one to get Paul Terry was a beauty – he opened him up like a can of beans and it hit the top of the middle and off stumps. Once we'd got through the first four batters, there wasn't a lot of resistance left. The odd ball kicked and I got a few to turn sharply. Steve McEwan did exactly what an opening bowler should do when they followed on. We always felt he'd get wickets today, because he's on a high and bowling really well. He has the ability to bowl several beauties in a row and, after a time, one of them will get a wicket. Macca can't believe how it's going for him. Whenever he gets a wicket we all gather round him saying, 'Well done!', and he just stands there, laughing. He grins, laughs, thanks us and then goes back to his mark, expecting to get another wicket with his next ball. Not a bad attitude to have when you're going for the title in mid-August.

Day Three – Hampshire 97 (Illingworth 5/23). Worcestershire won by an innings and 91 runs.

DILLEY:

It was all over just after lunch, with Illy taking five of the six wickets to fall today. Once Chris Smith was stumped, that was it, apart from a brief flurry from Malcolm Marshall. He hit Illy for three sixes, then put up an enormous skier that we thought Paul Bent would never catch. Benty had already dropped a couple of easier ones and as he stood at deep mid-on, trying to locate the swirler, not many of us were watching. He kept his nerve, and caught it with his arms outstretched. Funny how sides that are full of confidence hold horrible ones like that. If you take out those 18 runs off three strokes, Illy's analysis is remarkable – about half a run per over and a wicket every four overs. He's a handy, mean bowler to have around on a pitch like this, because he won't give anything away and he's just too fast in the air for them to get down the pitch to him.

HICK:

Illy loved today. When he sees something in the wicket for him, he never lets up. It's hard for a spinner these days. He rarely gets much bowling in May, and yet when he comes on a wicket like this later in the season, he's expected to clean up. Today will give Illy some consolation for his disappointment at Colchester last week. I've noticed this year from slip that Illy is giving the ball a little more air. We used to call him 'Eric' after Eric Bristow, because it seemed that he just wanted to dart the ball at the batter, but this year he's picked up one or two stumpings and he's getting better and better.

Meanwhile Essex beat Lancashire with just thirteen balls to spare, as the top two sides pulled away from the pack. Worcestershire, who had now won four of their last five games, had a fourteen-point advantage. They now needed just fifty-nine more points from their last three games to retain the title, a heartening prospect to take into the NatWest semi-final the following day at Edgbaston. They were now hot favourites for the 'double' of championship and NatWest Cup.

HICK:

I listened to the Essex news on the way back to Worcester and when I switched on the Teletext at home I had my fingers crossed that Lancashire might have held out – but fair play to Essex, they're hanging on and winning well. If we win two out of our last three, we should be there. I'm happy to have Glamorgan over four days at the end, because we should beat them over a long game and they might not be too committed at that stage of the season. Gloucestershire are a strong side on paper, but they seem to lack spirit, so we ought to beat them at home. Somerset should be the biggest problem, because they've got batsmen who love to occupy the crease. And Jimmy Cook surely won't fail twice again, will he?

DILLEY:

It's a nice position to be in. Of the three opponents, I'm more bothered about Somerset, but it's all in our hands. If we keep on winning, Essex will miss out. As for tomorrow, there's no real contest man for man between us and Warwickshire, but they're on a roll now after a few good wins and we've got injury problems. My knee gave out again on the final day at Bournemouth and I couldn't take the field. I don't hold out much chance for tomorrow – I think I'm going to have to ration myself to get through the championship games. Beefy has no chance after dislocating his finger in the Test and Radford is complaining about groin strain. We'll all have to be there early tomorrow for the fitness checks, but I can't see me playing.

Wednesday, August 16 – Warwickshire 220/9 (Moles 61, Asif Din 94 not out), Worcestershire 120. Warwickshire won by 100 runs and play Middlesex in the NatWest final.

HICK:

Another semi-final defeat. It happened to us twice in 1986 but it gets no easier to take, especially after playing as badly as we did today. Everything went wrong for us and they made it very difficult with their commitment and drive. But we would've won if we'd shown anything like our recent form. How can it have left us at the wrong time? I failed – caught behind off Dermot Reeve for 7 – and I know people will start saying that I can't handle the pressure of the big-match atmosphere and they'll hark back to when I got out in the final at Lord's last year. I think those who say that don't really know their cricket because I've done well in enough pressure situations, but I could do without such jibes at the moment.

I was annoyed at myself for agreeing to bat down the order. When our first wicket fell in the opening over, we sent Steve Rhodes in ahead of me. The scoring rate was never going to be a problem and the feeling was that Steve would blunt the attack and steal a few singles. I should've insisted I went out instead. Against Alan Donald and Gladstone Small you need the best batters in the side to combat the early blast and Steve would've been more useful lower down when we needed to pull the innings back our way. I wouldn't be much of a batter if I didn't fancy getting runs on that slow Edgbaston pitch. It was purely a tactical decision – but the wrong one. The local papers had built up the battle between me and Alan Donald and some must have thought I didn't fancy facing him with his tail up. When I got in, I hit a good off-drive when Donald bowled one in the right spot, but then Dermot Reeve got me out. The ball before, I had a wild slash and mishit it to the covers. Next ball pitched a foot outside and went wider after landing. I played what I thought was the perfect off-drive, except I nicked it. Everything seemed to be in the right place, with my bat coming through straight. Tonight Dolly told me that he couldn't understand how I nicked it, from where he was standing at the other end – and after watching it on the video, I feel the same. I had my mind set on a big contribution from me to help get us to Lord's and I could hear the Warwickshire fielders crowing as I walked off. I sat down in the dressing room feeling really disappointed with myself, but after I'd put my kit in the bag, I thought, 'We can still win this.' After all, Phil Neale was still there and we only needed just over 200. But then Phil was run out because he wasn't wearing spikes. The captain's always quick to have a go at Beefy when he wears rubbers, but Phil does the same when he bats. He's very quick on his feet from his football days and he feels constricted with spikes, but this time he slipped and was run out. As he walked back, we made a mental note to pull his leg about that when things are more cheerful. Then Dolly was out to a complete fluke when Paul Smith palmed a fierce shot to cover, who caught it. That just about summed up our day.

Out there Trevor Penny was fielding like a demon for them as substitute for the injured Alvin Kallicharran. I've played a fair bit of club cricket back home with Trevor and he's an absolutely brilliant fielder with a flat, accurate throw from his baseball days. Just our luck that Kalli was injured in his innings and they replaced a forty-year-old with someone like Trevor. Phil Neale was quite happy about that but I'm not so sure Andy Lloyd would've been as accommodating if the boot had been on the other foot. We used to struggle to get on a friendly footing with him. Perhaps it's because Warwickshire have been in our shadows for a long time and he felt it as captain. As they walked past our dressing room they were very loud, rubbing our noses in it intentionally, I thought. I know we've been boisterous when we've won something but not to the extent that we shouted our mouths off and bad-mouthed the opposition.

Where else did we go wrong? We gave them too many runs at the end of their innings by not bowling at one side of the wicket and spraying it around instead. Radford had hummed and hawed about playing and when he did decide to make himself available he bowled his twelve overs straight off before lunch. But he should've been bowling at the death when the slogging started. Perhaps seven overs at the start and five at the end would've been more valuable. They got about 30 too many at the end but you'd back yourself to get a total you face almost every Sunday with twenty extra overs available today. It was a slow wicket but we should be used to things like that. It was a blow losing Tim Curtis in the first over, because he is good at batting for a long time on slow wickets. Initially we thought he was unlucky to be adjudged lbw because at the moment everyone's appealing for that against Tim whenever the ball hits his pad. They've all seen him get out lbw in the Tests and they believe he's a candidate for that all the time now. TC thought the ball swung late down leg-side, but after seeing it on the highlights I think it was fairly close.

Long before the end we knew we were going to lose, so we had time to prepare ourselves. The captain said a few words afterwards about picking ourselves up for the championship and we went off to a pub near Droitwich to drown our sorrow. We shared a platter of scampi and chips, had a few beers and a bit of a laugh and tried to get it out of our system. It still hurts, though.

DILLEY:

I couldn't even run, so there was no chance of playing today. That made it even worse from the sidelines as we played so badly, so surprisingly badly. It was a pretty abysmal performance and I can't think of one redeeming feature. We can't offer injuries as an excuse because we've been doing very well recently with a weakened side and our confidence was very high. Gladstone Small and Alan Donald are a fine opening pair and we never got settled against them to build a proper score. We weren't allowed to up the tempo and we kept on losing wickets. They went bananas when they got Graeme out, which just shows their respect for his abilities, but these days his dismissal does more for the opposition than us. We just shrug and say 'Hicky's out,' fully expecting someone else to do the necessary for us. Today it didn't happen. The only enjoyable moment came at the end when they were singing their heads off and making a lot out of beating us. Geoff Humpage waddled past our dressing room, singing something about 'We're on our way to Lord's' and then Steve O'Shaughnessy came up with the perfect answer: 'We'll give you a bloody map because you've obviously forgotten the way down there.' We all burst out laughing and that helped create a better mood. Now to the future – and some rest for a couple of days. We all need it. It's been a hard, long month of continuous cricket but success and different locations have kept the boys going. We're very near the big prize now and I can't believe we'll blow it.

Sunday, 20 August – Worcestershire 202/5 (Hick 81), Somerset 190/7 (Marks 67 not out). Worcestershire won by 12 runs, to finish joint second in the Refuge Assurance League. They would now play Essex in the semi-final of the Refuge Cup at New Road.

 HICK:

Our bad start did for us in the Sunday league but we've kept plugging away and finishing second is no disgrace. It's ironic that we have to face Essex in the semi-final – we seem fated this summer. Today Jimmy Cook again failed and after that we coasted. Vic Marks played well in his nudging and nurdling way. He's a nice man – I'm sorry he's retiring because I like his infectious humour. He's a great giggler. Last year, when I scored my 405 not out against Somerset, I hit him for quite a few sixes. Today he got his revenge, hitting me for six over long-on, and when he next came down my end, he grinned and said, 'I still owe you another thirty-eight of them.' When we batted, I played well for my 81, but got out in the last few overs, hitting one straight up in the air. Dolly again batted well for his 47. It may not appear that he's had all that good a season but he's played very attractively in the last month, and at the start of the season he was the only one of our batters who shaped up at all on the New Road pitches. He's the kind of batsman who likes to play his shots early, but all he needs to do is curb his enthusiasm a fraction when he comes in.

Tonight Paul Pridgeon and I had a pretty heated discussion in the bar. Pridge wanted me to play in three successive benefit games before our next match, the important one against Somerset that we want to win badly. Pridge hasn't been travelling with us because of his injury and I told him he had no idea how tired we all were. He conveniently forgot that he's had us driving to different parts of the country to support him in benefit functions, and that we didn't need too much of that after a long slog in the county games. I told him I'd rather just play two of the three games and have a totally free day, which I felt was perfectly reasonable, but he wouldn't have it. I'm annoyed at him, because he should know what the last month has been like. He's been on the staff for long enough. It all got out of proportion because of fatigue and tension. When you've had two days off in the past month, things do get on top of you. Now I'm home I've been sat in front of the telly like a zombie, just relaxing. I've been watching anything from old black-and-white films to kids' programmes. I haven't really been following the programmes, but it's helped to relax me, letting the events of the last month wash all over me. I know that I've got to raise my game over the last fortnight – we mustn't chuck away all our hard work now.

Thursday, 24 August. Somerset 256/8 (Tavaré 89).

HICK:

When Tavaré took root, we had to keep telling ourselves that this is a four-day game, to keep calm and just concentrate on winkling him out. The wicket played well – possibly too well – and it was hard work for the bowlers on just about the best wicket we've seen at New Road this season. It might be hard to bowl them out twice to win this one, because we're without Botham, Dilley, Radford, Newport and Pridgeon – an entire pace attack. It could well be a declaration job, with a stiff target for us on the final afternoon. We got Jimmy Cook cheaply again. He looks tired and Stu Lampitt got him halfway in the crease to one that came back off the seam. I struggle to judge lbws from second slip, but Stuey said he was plumb. Have you ever heard a bowler say it wasn't plumb? I got Jonathan Atkinson out in an amusing way. He smacked one back at me off the bottom of the bat and I stuck up my hand in reflex action. Somehow the ball plopped in my hand and I just stood there, staring at it. I thought it would've come back to me at far greater speed.

Day Two – Somerset 300/8.

 HICK:

Only eighteen overs bowled all day. Just our luck, after such a wonderful summer, that the weather looks like breaking just as we're in the home stretch. I'll be surprised if Somerset declare overnight, because they owe us nothing and they must play the game properly on behalf of the other counties. When we do get in, I suspect we'll have to declare behind and hope they'll set us a target. Just as well it's a four-day game.

Day Three – Somerset 338, Worcestershire 200/5 dec. (Hick 86, D'Oliveira 63).

 HICK:

The wicket is still playing well, so we had to declare behind and hope for something from them. Again I got out in the 80s when I should've got a hundred. It was a great catch by Graham Rose at slip, though – diving back to his left to take one-handed a very fast edge. I'd have been very happy with that one if I'd been at slip. As for the game, our only hope is a fine day and a challenging declaration.

Day Four – Somerset 151/6 dec. (Tavaré 62), Worcestershire 302/5 (Hick 136 not out, Curtis 84). Worcestershire won by five wickets.

 HICK:

Today I've played my best innings of the summer and the fact that it might also have won us the championship makes it even better. Vic Marks made a good declaration, asking us to get 300 and giving himself fifty-seven overs to bowl us out. He did us no favours and we deserved to win because we paced our effort so well. Tim Curtis and I had another of our partnerships and again the balance was right. We ran a lot of ones and twos, working the ball around and pouncing on anything loose. At one stage the target got up to nine and over, and TC and I agreed that 120 off the last fifteen overs was gettable as long as we didn't lose many wickets. We felt we hadn't got many boundaries for a long time but when we got to 170-odd we realised we were on target for the final push. All those ones and twos added up. At tea we were still together and I felt very confident. I looked over at the captain and he looked very pensive. I told him not to worry, I was really fired up.

TC got out when he was going very well and after a short and sweet nought from Dolly the captain came in and picked up the tempo. By now I was looking for sixes and striking the ball well. I pulled Rose for six over mid-wicket off the meat of the bat, picked Mallender off my legs for four then next ball he tried to bowl a slower one. It pitched short and I helped it on its way to backward square leg for six. I was surprised to see it soar into the crowd. The bat I'm using is a belter, with a lot of wood high up on the blade so it swings easily. I use a short handle because I prefer to feel the weight near to my hands rather than further down the blade. During this innings I realised what lovely balance was in that bat. I couldn't believe it when I swung Jones over mid-wicket for six. I picked him up at the last moment and it didn't feel right on the bat. I looked up and saw it going over the longest part of the boundary! Afterwards everybody told me it looked such a nonchalant shot, but I really tried to belt it. I mishit that ball for six. By now I was really motoring, running purely on adrenalin. I had to take risks, yet I didn't think I was going to get out. Vic Marks tried containing me by pitching his off-breaks on the leg-stump, but I managed to get inside them and play him through the off-side. The crowd got bigger and bigger and I was really excited at the atmosphere. Steve Rhodes hit the winning runs – a crashing square cut – and we were overjoyed when we walked off.

It was one of the best innings of my career. The importance of it was obvious. I didn't give a chance and I paced it just right. You have to approach it in stages, you can't go in and expect to crash it around at nine an over right away. I get a lot of pleasure out of personal performances but if they help to win the match, that's even better. It was a great thrill to catch sight of my team-mates as I got near to the pavilion. If you're going to bat for any reason, it's for the respect of your team-mates. I value that more than anything, because they know how hard it is out there and only they know the difficult times we've had. It was also great to walk into the members' bar afterwards with everyone shaking my hand, slapping me on the back, with me struggling to get to the bar. A perfect day.

DILLEY:

That was an absolutely unbelievable innings. At tea we were a bit edgy but Graeme said, 'Don't worry, we'll get them.' He seemed so confident and he played like it. The way he found the gaps was brilliant and he paced it all so well. Somerset played it exactly the right way – they used proper bowlers and tried to get us out. Essex can't complain that a great batsman got us to a stiff target. All we need now is for them to lose at Northants and we're home and dry.

They did. Next day Northants beat Essex by four wickets. That meant Worcestershire needed only to beat Gloucestershire in the next match at New Road to retain the title. With Dilley and Botham back after injury, it seemed a foregone conclusion.
Tuesday, 29 August. Day One – Worcestershire 240/8 (Curtis 98).

DILLEY:

We're not going to get maximum batting points, but that won't matter as long as we win. It's not a great wicket, it's very slow, but there's no danger of getting docked twenty-five points. We needed Tim Curtis to bat all day and he almost did. In the end the crowd got him out. It was getting dark, Courtney Walsh was bowling well at one end and David Graveney at the other and TC went into his shell. That wouldn't have mattered because we have four days to play this match, but Tim then got out. Again he took far too much notice of what people have been saying. The ones who barracked him are the ones who've been influenced by the commentators who say Curtis isn't up to it because he plays with a crooked bat. Tim should play his own way for now and worry about that in the winter. We keep telling him that if he gets a single at the start of an over, leaving Graeme Hick to smash a four, that's five an over and doing very nicely. Tim is just too sensitive.

HICK:

Another valuable innings by TC. If only he realised how much he's respected by the rest of the team, he wouldn't then need to worry about getting the slow handclap. Because of him we might get a decent score. I was out lbw to Curran and I almost walked for it. I had a sudden mental block and my foot didn't move. The ball was well pitched up and I like to think that on other days I would've whipped it through mid-wicket for four. That brought me back down to earth after my knock against Somerset – perhaps I subconsciously relaxed too much. Today it was a case of spending time at the crease rather than a high-adrenalin effort, and I wasn't concentrating hard enough. Beefy came and went quickly after hitting three good boundaries. He needs to get into the nets and work hard before next season starts. Bowlers need to get through a certain amount of overs every season to be at their best and batters are no different. Beefy's not getting runs because he's not spending time at practice or in the middle.

Day Two – Worcestershire 248 and 62/2, Gloucestershire 206 (Alleyne 55, McEwan 5/61). Worcestershire lead by 104 runs.

DILLEY:

The most important event of the day was that G. R. Dilley got yet another not-out. As I keep telling my batting colleagues, nobody's good enough to dismiss me these days. I must be well on the way to an average of more than 20 this season, and well deserved that is too. As for the game, we're not home and dry by any means. We lost two unnecessary wickets near the end tonight, when we'd already turned down the offer of the light. The wicket is all right – it's seamed around a bit and there's always the hope that eventually you'll come up with a ball good enough to get a man out. The umpires said we hadn't batted well enough, that it wasn't a 240-ish wicket, and I think they're right. I bowled quite well today and I was pleased to do Curran with the slower ball. When I get it right the ball also swings a little and this time it did: he lost his balance and got a little inside edge on it. For long periods today, we've had the upper hand but I'm still concerned at the way we let them back into it. We ought to have a lead of a hundred on first innings.

HICK:

For me Curran was the danger man and it was a great piece of bowling from Dill that did him completely. They don't look a happy side, they're full of cliques and there are rumours that Bill Athey is going to pack in the captaincy after just one season. So they're there for the taking but we're making heavy weather of it. Now we have to pile up the runs tomorrow and look to bowl them out on the last day.

Day Three – Worcestershire 213, Gloucestershire 124 (Dilley 4/22). Worcestershire won by 131 runs to retain the championship.

DILLEY:

These thoughts are the-morning-after-the-night-before thoughts, because I got drunk pretty rapidly last night. It was amazing that it all came together in about half an hour when it looked as if they were going to make us work very hard. They needed 256 to win and it should've been more but we didn't apply ourselves with the bat. After a reasonable start they collapsed and I'm glad to say that I mopped up the tail in time-honoured fashion. I owed that to the lads for all their support of me this summer. Last year, when Richard Illingworth took the wicket to give us the title, I remember thinking, 'That must be a nice feeling.' Last night I had the honour, as Illy took a bloody good effort running back from mid-off. Afterwards he said all he could think about was £35,000 in prize money dropping into his hands: once a Yorkie, always a Yorkie!

If you wanted tension and excitement, well it was better last year when it went to the last day, but we're not complaining that we wrapped it up a day early. My mind went back to last April when I told Duncan Fearnley after we'd beaten Notts, 'Eleven more of those and we've won the title.' Normally twelve wins is enough. I felt a great sense of relief that I'd managed to get through the last month and be there to play a significant role when it was most needed. I thought about that semi-final defeat at Edgbaston and realised that some clubs would have settled for that from their season. Great for our team and also for the club's long-term future. Stuey Lampitt and Steve McEwan were capped on the balcony as soon as we came off the field and that was a nice gesture. Having come in at a crucial time and won us matches they deserved recognition and security. I believe we're now the best team in the country, despite what Essex may say. I wonder how they would have coped with our injuries.

⊖ HICK:

I didn't think we had enough runs, so I was absolutely delighted when they folded. Beefy and Steve Rhodes were always confident we'd do it, but they always are anyway. I was really pleased for Dill – he bowled superbly towards the end and made sure they wouldn't get a sniff. He turned the game in just a couple of overs. We shan't forget the way he's battled on this season when never really fit to play. It was a great feeling to be out there with the last pair together, just waiting for that final wicket in the sunshine. A few guys grabbed the stumps at the end but I'll wait for something like that till I'm older: I hope there'll be plenty of days like this one before I'm finished. I'm particularly delighted for Phil Neale. He'd had a hard season, battling with his own form and having to deal with criticism of our wickets. There's always the worry about his son as well – leukaemia takes a long time to recover from.

Sometimes Phil can be a little snappy in the dressing room, but that's because he's such a professional and likes to have peace and quiet at the right times. I find I have the same approach and ideals as Phil, and I have the greatest respect for him. We simply aren't the same side when he's not with us on the field.

I don't normally suffer from hangovers but this morning I'm suffering. After the usual champagne, we ended up in a wine bar and the owner kindly slipped us into the back room to carry on drinking after closing time. Then it was off to our favourite Chinese restaurant and more celebrations. Quite an assault on the digestive system. Mind you, players from sixteen other counties would give anything to feel as badly as I do this morning. It was in a very good cause.

ANTI-CLIMAX IN SEPTEMBER

Worcestershire played just three first-team games in September and none of them yielded a great deal of satisfaction. A match at Scarborough for the Ward Trophy, a semi-final in the Refuge Cup and a four-day championship encounter at rain-sodden Pontypridd added up to a rather low-key end to the season. In contrast, September 1988 had featured an appearance in the NatWest Final at Lord's and the destination of the championship pennant had been in doubt until 16 September, when Worcestershire had beaten Glamorgan, to pip Kent by a single point.
Monday, 4 September – Worcestershire 221/4 off fifty overs (Curtis 95, Weston 64), Essex 222/2 (Gooch 76, Hardie 86). Essex won by eight wickets and play Yorkshire in the Ward Trophy Final.

HICK:

A pleasant enough trip. We went up the night before and had a few drinks with the Essex lads. They seemed fine about losing the championship to us – they didn't say anything about losing twenty-five points because they knew that basically that was nothing to do with us. We didn't play very well against them next day – there was a bit of a festive spirit. We would've liked to get back at them after the draw at Colchester but they played better. It's a pity the draw pitted us against each other, leaving Leicestershire to play Yorkshire, because we were after all the two best sides in the country. We can't get away from Essex – we see them again in two days' time at Worcester for the Refuge Cup semi.

Wednesday, 6 September – Essex 211/7 (Prichard 82 not out), Worcestershire 110. Essex won by 101 runs and play Nottinghamshire in the Refuge Cup Final.

172

DILLEY:

I never had a chance of playing because of the knee. We're now trying to fix up a visit to the surgeon, because I want to get it sorted out as soon as possible, then start training hard for South Africa. I suppose it's understandable we performed badly today, because a sense of anti-climax is bound to be there after winning the title so early. It's not that the lads didn't want to play well, but more a subconscious thing. We had a full house, and Essex always provide a competitive edge, but it just wasn't there. My old mate John Lever picked up a few wickets, including Graeme for a duck. Always good to have a chinwag with J.K. He's retiring next week, but I bet he'll still be fit enough to play for them in an emergency.

HICK:

They did us quite easily in the end, and that seemed to mean a lot to them. We didn't consciously think this game was an irritating extra after a hard season – it helps the sponsors, our home crowd would've been happy if we'd beaten Essex and it would've meant another cup final. We wanted to win as much as our supporters but we just couldn't raise our game. Perhaps Essex were hungrier and the saga of the twenty-five points gave them something to get pumped up about. They've had a very successful season, but so far they haven't won anything, so the Refuge Cup would mean a fair amount to them, I suppose. My nought was through a bad shot: I pushed a drive at a wide one, caught it halfway up on the outside of the bat and was caught at point.

Two days later, the England selectors had completed their deliberations on three winter tours and there were several shocks. Predictably, David Gower was sacked as England captain and replaced by Graham Gooch for the short tour to India and then to the West Indies next January. Although Phil Neale had been widely touted for the England job, he missed out and he was also passed over in favour of Mark Nicholas for the England 'A' leadership to Zimbabwe. There was some consolation for Worcestershire – Richard Illingworth and Steve Rhodes were picked for the 'A' tour. But the biggest surprises concerned Ian Botham and David Gower. They were both omitted from the West Indies tour party 'purely on cricketing grounds', according to the selectors.

DILLEY:

Gower is still our best player and he had to go to the West Indies. There shouldn't be any other reason for his selection and I just wonder what other forces have been at work. It wasn't a closely guarded secret that he and Micky Stewart didn't see eye to eye this summer, nor have they done so since Micky came on board in Australia in 1986/7. It's ridiculous to say that David is out because of current form, because only Robin Smith scored more runs in this last series. David is not a difficult person to deal with and you have to pick your best players for the West Indies, whatever the complexities. He plays quick bowling so well and I'd back him to get more runs out there than most of them. He has to come back because of his great ability, but it'll take him a while to get over his disenchantment. I also think Beefy will come back: he's only thirty-four and he's got very little competition for the all-rounder's spot. I see a different role for him, because he won't be the third seamer, but he has so much talent. I would've debated Beefy's selection for a long time but after deliberation I would've taken him and given him a specific role, possibly as vice-captain or in charge of the youngsters. He does have a lot to offer if handled in the right way. He would have needed responsibility on that tour.

On balance I would have stayed with Gower as captain. To my mind there were only two possible candidates because of their stature as players – Gower and Gooch. Over there you just can't afford to carry anyone, and it would be preferable to have one or two Tests go into the fifth day. This last Test series wasn't all David's fault – the players let him down. One bad series shouldn't mean the sack. What about continuity? Is this change just for the sake of change? Why not do like the Aussies did with Allan Border – have a five-year plan but don't tell the public and hope the captain grows into the job? Especially as Gower is still the best batsman in the side.

I don't think Phil Neale should have had the England job, because I'm not sure how good initially he'd be on the wider stage. He's not quite in the right class as a batsman and to me he's perfect for Worcestershire, but might be out of his depth with England. You need your eleven best available players for the West Indies, and I don't think Phil could honestly lay claim to a place in the first six batters.

I think Ricky Elcock is good choice for the senior tour, because he's quick, knows the Caribbean and should be fresh. Alec Stewart deserves his chance after scoring a lot of runs for Surrey. Wayne Larkins is a good choice – he has it in him to destroy any attack and he knows that at his age this is his last chance. Talent has never been his problem. I wouldn't have taken bright young players like Nasser Hussain or Keith Medlycott because they have a lot ahead of them and they shouldn't be exposed too early to the special demands of a West Indies tour. For the same reason it was right to spare Mike Atherton. A bad time in the Caribbean can set a young player back several seasons, so I would have taken players who were expendable – like David Smith and Gehan Mendis. These are players who will just see you through the series, who will fight it out and do a short-term job. Just two openers – perhaps another ten will be needed!

I can't quarrel with many of the 'A' team selections, although I think Phil Neale might have been a worthwhile choice as captain. I don't see the sense in taking Derek Pringle, because they know what he can and can't do. Apart from that, no complaints. The Leicestershire boys tell me that Chris Lewis is a great prospect. I rate Atherton, both the Bicknells and Richard Blakey. Steve Watkin was unlucky to miss out on the West Indies tour and he deserves this trip for all the hard work he put in this summer.

 HICK:

I think Phil Neale deserved to lead the 'A' tour. He never even received a letter asking him if he was available as a player, which was hard. Phil would've been very good with the younger players in Zimbabwe. Mark Nicholas has got runs this year and he has his supporters at Lord's. He and Phil have more or less the same batting record, although Mark is probably the more stylish player. The fact that he took the English Counties side out there must have counted for a lot. I'm surprised they've made Atherton the vice-captain. I know he's very mature but at a similar age I wouldn't want to be saddled with such a responsibility when I'm still making my way as a player. He's now under immediate pressure. You don't make England captains – it's just bred into you. It's not like telling a good schoolboy player what he has to do when he leads the side. At international level, you can't coach captaincy into someone.

Gower's omission really surprised me. His form stood up well in the Tests, and he's still one of the best batsmen available. I was less surprised that Beefy missed out. He hasn't performed well enough, even though he has had his injury problems. I think he'll be back in the England side next year though, if only to put two fingers up at everyone who has written him off. No one will fill his place for a long time to come – they'll need two people to do the job he's done for so many years.

As usual in September, it was time to say farewell to players who were no longer part of the club's plans. This season at Worcester, Paul Pridgeon was not re-engaged after seventeen years on the staff, while Steve O'Shaughnessy will be playing league cricket next year back in Lancashire.

HICK:

It would've been nice if Pridge could have stayed on for another season after his benefit. It would've been wrong if he had kept out young bowlers like Lampitt and McEwan, but there would surely be a place for him if we suffer injuries and Test calls. Only last year, Pridge was top of the Sunday league averages and if he shook off that Achilles problem, he would still have something to offer. He and I are fine now after our spat a few weeks ago – I just wanted to get it out of my system. It sounds as if he will take a generous benefit with him into retirement.

▭━ DILLEY:

I'm surprised that Pridge isn't being retained. The cupboard might be pretty bare if Newport and Botham get picked for England and I continue to miss games through my dodgy knee. Lampitt and McEwan have done very well for us this season, but inexperienced seamers often suffer a reaction in their second full season. Achilles tendons are a problem as you get older, but Pridge is naturally fit and he's got the whole of the winter to get over that. He'll be missed on the field and in the dressing room. Every time I look at the *Sporting Life* I'll think of Pridge. Steve O'Shaughnessy's sense of humour kept us going during the bad times. He's a very funny man and his sense of humour appealed to me, because he often didn't realise he was being funny. He'll do all right for himself in the leagues.

Wednesday, 13 September. Day One – Glamorgan 221/7, at Pontypridd.

◯ HICK:

We were told when we got here this morning that there was no chance of getting a full four-day game in, because of the weather forecast. So we don't expect to get the win that would allow us to lead Essex by more than twenty-five points. Today we haven't been very impressive in the field. We dropped a few behind the wicket and the captain gave us a few black looks as if we'd had a heavy session last night (not true). We were joking about getting a lurid tie with a logo on it about a dropped catch, so that every day the guy who'd dropped one would have to wear it. Beefy thought that was a great idea because he was out at third man with his finger injury and unlikely to spill many out there. A couple of overs later, he was brought into gully. One whizzed past his left and he didn't go for it, but, next over, one went straight at him and he dropped it. We said, 'The tie's in the post, Beefy!'

The only impressive piece of cricket today came from Matthew

Maynard, who played very well for his 44, then got himself out. They say that's the trouble with him. Perhaps if he was with another county he would be welcomed back to the dressing room in stony silence when he gets himself out for a classy 50. To win trophies, your top batters have to do more than make half-centuries.

DILLEY:

I'm nowhere near fit enough to play but, after a fitness test, I'm in. But the knee gave out again and I hobbled off after lunch just as it was getting darker. I don't think I'll be the only player sitting around over the next few days – the forecast is awful.

Just half an hour's play was possible next day (Glamorgan 230/9) and then it rained and rained. There was no play on the final two days, so Worcestershire ended their championship season just six points ahead of Essex. It was a frustrating end for Graeme Hick: he started the game needing 176 more runs to reach 2000 runs in first-class cricket for the season, but he never got the opportunity.

HICK:

I would have been very keen on trying to get those runs. It was a four-day game, after all, and I have a good record against Glamorgan. It was also disappointing not to put some distance between ourselves and Essex, but I suppose that even if we had won, they would have said that they'd never recovered from the blow of losing those twenty-five points at the start of August.

We had a few laughs as we waited for each day's play to be abandoned. The Glamorgan boys are a sociable bunch and we went to a benefit function at a brewery for Rodney Ontong, which was no hardship! There was very little to do in the evenings in Pontypridd, and we played computer golf in the hotel bar. We must have put about £100 in that machine, pressing different buttons for a drive or a wedge and, by the time the trip was over, we were shooting three or four under par. The highlight of a damp few days!

ANTI-CLIMAX IN SEPTEMBER

DILLEY:

All we could do was make our own entertainment and hope for
an early abandonment. It was a novel feeling to watch the rain
pour down in this summer of drought. You tend to forget that
many an hour has been spent waiting for the umpires to squelch
back from the middle. This year there's been hardly any of that –
perhaps that's why the lads are so tired. The public may always
want to see us out there, but sometimes in a hard season you're
quite happy to open the curtains and see the rain tippling down in
the morning. So this was a fairly subdued trip, and the feeling of
anti-climax won't go away. By now we've all had enough and
thoughts turn to social matters. Will Pridgeon and Curtis organise
our end-of-season party with their customary efficiency?

AUTUMNAL REFLECTIONS

Hick and Dilley would both be in Africa at the start of 1990: Hick visiting his family in Zimbabwe, Dilley with Mike Gatting's side in South Africa. Hick flew off from Worcester in mid-November, relishing the prospect of meeting the new arrival in his close-knit family. Some serious fishing, a spot of gentle club cricket and a rendezvous with Steve Rhodes and Richard Illingworth when England 'A' arrived in Zimbabwe all suggested a pleasant few months. He could look back on a satisfying 1989 season, despite his early-season worries. A total of 1824 first-class runs, an average of 57, some useful wickets and the highest number of catches by a fielder (forty-three) and the most sixes by a batsman (twenty-nine) hardly suggest the decline of a great power. Only Jimmy Cook scored more first-class runs and centuries than Hick.

HICK:

Considering all that we went through, I was very happy with the end product. I scored almost a thousand runs in August and it meant a lot to me to find some form when the side really needed the contributions from me in the last few games. I'm proud of that innings against Somerset which won us the game. The context and the performance made it special for me. I now realise I didn't need to get all uptight about the wickets at New Road. It's a long season and far too early to be in despair by the middle of May. I hope the experience of 1989 has made me tougher mentally. I cringe at missing out on several hundreds by getting out in the 70s and 80s and I shall try to make amends next season. I shan't be going up and down the batting order, either: that experience in the NatWest semi-final taught me that you should stay in the same place. It felt odd that so many expected me to go out one day and get another 405 not out. I hope I have another chance to get somewhere near that, but if it never happens that's something to look back on with satisfaction. But it's not all about high scores. I'd rather be in the team that wins the county championship than get 200 for a side that's just coasting along.

The captain keeps getting letters with Essex postmarks saying we've won the title by default, but there's nothing we can do about that. We suffered more than anyone at New Road in May and June and there's no doubt that that hangover affected our performances both home and away in the first two months. Don't forget that seven of our twelve championship wins came away from New Road. It got to a stage where the opposition preferred playing at Worcester. Essex were caught out. They knew the score. We also battled away against a terrible run of injuries. At times we went into vital games without our usual seam attack. How would Essex have done without Foster, Pringle, Topley and Gooch? They had a few Test calls – but Gooch dropped out of the England team at Trent Bridge to play in two county games, while Pringle only played two Tests, Foster three and Stephenson one. We had just as many Test calls and far more injuries. It was good for the future of this club that we came through with young stand-ins who are local lads. That kind of thing gives them an even greater sense of pride, and you could see what it meant to the likes of McEwan, Lampitt, Bent and Tolley to be part of the set-up. They were a great shot in the arm when we needed a boost in July.

I thought Dill did remarkably well to get through the last month with another knee operation hanging over his head. I've no idea how many more he can take before having to quit but he never moaned about it, just got on quietly with the job. He gave us a lot of entertainment in May when he was training so hard to get fit again, but we also respected the amount of effort he was putting in. When he got on the pitch he did what every class strike bowler is expected to do – win us games. He won the games at Northampton and Old Trafford and made a vital contribution in the match against Gloucestershire that won us the title. All the time he was capable of getting the best players out with a great delivery that swung late, or that clever slower one. It's an education standing at slip watching Dill bowl and I hope he can get through a few more seasons with us. Not only is he a matchwinner but he's a genuine team man. I admit that my misgivings of 1987 were totally unfounded. Considering all the problems he's had, he's been brilliant for us.

Despite his fitness worries, his occasional lapses in form and his disappointing performances for England, Dilley could allow himself some pleasure from the 1989 season. He may have played just twelve of Worcestershire's twenty-two championship games, but he took fifty-five wickets for them, a total bettered only by Neal Radford. In all first-class cricket, a strike rate of a wicket every seven overs is more than satisfactory for a fast bowler. After his third knee operation in October within a year, Dilley felt optimistic about the remainder of his career.

DILLEY:

I've just been reading about an American footballer who's had nine knee operations. He's been advised to pack it in but he believes in modern technology and that science will eventually come up with something that'll solve his problem. I'm beginning to think along those lines. Knee operations don't have the fear factor of the past. You don't need stitches now. The surgeon can clean you out every six months, and there's not as much damage done to the tissues as there used to be. I'll keep having the operation if it sets me up for the season, but if I'm told to retire, that'll be it. Most fast bowlers go suddenly and that'll probably apply to me. I have two years left on my contract at Worcester and I hope to play till I'm around thirty-six. A lot depends on what the club want. Ideally it would help if I didn't play on Sundays, but much will depend on the fitness of others. It's very unlikely that I'll get through an entire season unscathed, but as long as I keep enjoying my cricket with Worcestershire I'd like to carry on. It may be that I'm in for a period of comparative obscurity now that I'm no longer an England player and that would be nice. Although most of the folk are perfectly pleasant, I've never enjoyed being buttonholed and looked at just because I am a certain person.

I'll still follow England and want them to beat everyone out of sight. I wish I could've done this winter's tour to the West Indies, then retired from internationals after the World Cup in Australasia in '91, but it wasn't to be. There was never a moment's hesitation over South Africa – the money was too good. Letters to me are running around fifty/fifty at the moment and I've had just one that was abusive. I was last out there in '85 and I expect to see a few changes. I can't imagine things have changed that much for the average black guy in the townships but at least the Government seem to be moving in the right direction and cricket deserves some credit for that. I do agree with people like Alan Boesak and Desmond Tutu that the system is wrong, and I just hope it will be overturned in a non-violent way. Any decent person would side with the aims of the anti-Apartheid movement, although I disagree with some of their methods.

This has been one of the most significant summers of my career, a time when I had to make important decisions. I know I've learned to handle setbacks better – I just tell myself this job pays the bills and try to enjoy as much of it as I can. You've got to go through adversity to appreciate the good times. Now that I'm just going to be a county player I believe I'll enjoy my cricket even more. It was a desperate summer for England, for David Gower and for myself against the Aussies and I still can't believe we were that bad. I tried my best, but it wasn't good enough. From now on I shall be more philosophical about setbacks like that – I shan't be so hard on myself as long as I keep trying. I'll never get a hundred first-class wickets in a summer because I won't be able to play all that many games. It would've been nice to see that in a little column when I've finished, but the success of the club is more important.

Since I came to Worcester, I haven't learned all that much about cricket that I didn't already know, but I've learned a lot about being a cricketer, about playing for the team and supporting each other, about being happy for a team-mate's success. I've got out of the syndrome that I'm an England bowler and that it's important to ration myself in the county games and keep most of it back for the Tests. All that's really bothered me since I came to Worcester in '87 has been doing my very best for my county. Playing for England was a bonus because I have loved playing cricket at Worcester. I desperately want to do well for them as long as I can and I suppose my major consolation from 1989 must be that I did my job for them whenever I could. In my last couple of years at Kent, I was very unhappy. Things went on that I couldn't abide – like playing Derek Aslett in the first half of the season, then giving the other half to Neil Taylor and dropping Aslett after he'd done well. Where was the incentive to succeed? Chris Tavaré was the best captain in England in 1984, then he got sacked. All they ever wanted was a Cowdrey running the side again. Coming to Worcester has been a massive relief to me. The fact that we see each other such a lot on days off indicates how well we get on as mates, and our management team at New Road is first-class. They treat us like adults and common sense is also lightened with humour.

There were so many decisive moments in the season. Getting off to a good start at Trent Bridge helped – that's where I made my first confident forecast that we would win the title again. The freshness and surprising skills of McEwan and Lampitt. The solid grafting of Neale and Illingworth at Bournemouth, when the wicket was obviously breaking up. Hicky's wonderful innings that won the Somerset game. Phil Neale's return to the captaincy in the nick of time after jaundice. But I think getting away from New Road in mid-season and calling in Harry Brind were crucial. After that it would've been very hard if we'd been docked twenty-five points because we worked so hard to improve our pitches with Harry's help.

As for Graeme Hick, it's a tribute to his excellence that people kept talking about him having a poor season. If that was true, credit should be given to the others for making up for his alleged poor form. But it wasn't true. To average over 50 in this summer of dodgy pitches and Reader balls was a tremendous achievement. He sets such high standards that he's not the only one disappointed when he appears human. I defy anyone to play any better than he did when he beat Somerset more or less off his own bat at the end of August. That was a high-pressure innings, but he was so calm and positive – a huge inspiration to the rest of us. Graeme will score heaps of runs next season and the experience of having to work very hard for everything this year will make him an even better player. I wish I could walk out with him when he first plays for England in 1991, but that's another matter.

What impressed me even more about him this year was that he didn't show any moodiness even though he was falling below his standards. Other players can be very bitchy and sulky when they're having a bad time, but you would never have known from the way Graeme conducted himself that he was down. He must be very tight mentally, because he wouldn't show the disappointment that I'm certain he was feeling. He kept saying the right, diplomatic things whenever a well-intentioned supporter asked him why he wasn't getting as many runs as last year, and he still joined in all the dressing-room banter. Graeme has a great sense of responsibility to the team, unlike many other star players I've known. That is one of the reasons why he is both so popular and respected so much.

So it's another round of hard training for me throughout this autumn. More white wine and soda. For me the stakes are just as high as they were in May, when I was battling to get back into Worcester's first team and, if possible, the England side. The South Africans will be very tough to beat because they've been starved of representative cricket and they won't slacken off for a second. A lot will depend on how much time we'll get out there to acclimatise and practise after having had four months off. I hope I'll still be able to locate the stumps when I first run up to bowl! I fully expect our team spirit to be excellent. We have the right leader in Mike Gatting and the fact that we are unpopular in some areas will only serve to keep us together. If our morale and sense of humour can be anywhere near what we had at Worcester in the 1989 season, that will be more than enough.

STATISTICAL APPENDIX

Key to abbreviations:
BAC   Britannic Assurance Championship
BH   Benson and Hedges Cup
NW   NatWest Bank Trophy
RAL   Refuge Assurance League
RAC   Refuge Assurance Cup
TT   Tilcon Trophy
WF   Ward Four County Knock-out Cup
OF   Other first-class match
★   Not out

15–18 April – OF – Lord's – *v*. MCC – Worcs 474/3 dec., MCC
281/4. Match drawn.
Hick 173★, Dilley 16–6–58–0

20–24 April – BAC – Trent Bridge – *v*. Nottinghamshire –
Notts 218 and 198, Worcs 291 and 129/3. Worcs won by 7 wkts.
Dilley 20.3–0–42–5 and 14.4–4–40–2, Hick 56 and 55★,
Dilley 4

23 April – RAL – Trent Bridge – *v*. Nottinghamshire – Match
abandoned. No result.

26 April – BH – Lord's – *v*. Middlesex – Worcs 115/6, Middx
114/7. Worcs won by one run.
Hick 21, Dilley 6–0–23–1

27–30 April – BAC – Edgbaston – *v*. Warwickshire – Worcs
143 and 160/5 dec., Warwicks 99 and 204/6. Match drawn.

Hick 7 and 5, Dilley 12–5–28–5 and 14–2–45–1

2 May – BH – Oval – *v*. Surrey – Worcs 190/7, Surrey 191/9.
Surrey won by one wkt.
Hick 24, Dilley 11–1–28–3, Hick 2–0–15–0

4–6 May – BAC – New Road – *v*. Lancashire – Lancs 171 and
231, Worcs 166 and 170. Lancs won by 66 runs.
Dilley 13–2–41–3 and 16.1–2–62–4, Hick 15 and 2, Dilley O★
and 5★

7 May – RAL – New Road – *v*. Lancashire – Lancs 202/8, Worcs
188/9. Lancs won by 14 runs.
Hick 4

9 May – BH – New Road – *v*. Gloucestershire – Gloucs 200/7,
Worcs 152. Gloucs won by 48 runs.
Hick 16

11 May – BH – New Road – *v*. Combined Universities – Worcs
216/8, Universities 217/5. Universities won by five wkts.
Hick 109 and 8–0–35–0

13–14 May – OF – New Road – *v*. Australians – Australians 103
and 205, Worcs 146 and 163/7. Worcs won by three wkts.
Hick 13 and 43

21 May – RAL – New Road – *v*. Surrey – Surrey 221/5, Worcs
216/8. Surrey won by five runs.
Hick 1

24–26 May – BAC – New Road – *v*. Nottinghamshire – Worcs
209 and 180/3 dec., Notts 150/3 dec. and 238/9. Match drawn.
Hick 9 and 90★, 7–2–21–0 and 2–0–18–0

27–30 May – BAC – Bristol – *v*. Gloucestershire – Worcs 201
and 283/6 dec., Gloucs 148 and 257. Worcs won by 79 runs.
Hick 8 and 53

28 May – RAL – Bristol – *v*. Gloucestershire – Gloucs 221/5, Worcs 222/4. Worcs won by six wkts.
Hick 84

3–5 June – BAC – New Road – *v*. Glamorgan – Worcs 127 and 246/3 dec., Glamorgan 134 and 20/0. Match drawn.
Hick 43 and 0

4 June – RAL – New Road – *v*. Glamorgan – Worcs 262/4, Glamorgan 119. Worcs won by 143 runs.
Hick 50

10–13 June – BAC – New Road – *v*. Derbyshire – Worcs 220 and 227/8, Derbys 157 and 145. Worcs won by 145 runs.
Hick 17 and 42, Dilley 8★ and 11★, 21.2–9–42–5 and 14.1–4–51–1

11 June – RAL – New Road – *v*. Derbyshire – Worcs 207/6, Derbys 177. Worcs won by 30 runs.
Hick 6 and 7–0–44–2, Dilley 5–0–11–0

14 June – TT Semi-Final – Harrogate – *v*. Sussex – Sussex 170 all out, Worcs 249. Worcs won by 79 runs.
Hick 80 and 11–1–41–3, Dilley 9–3–13–1

15 June – TT Final – Harrogate – *v*. Surrey – Surrey 225/7, Worcs 226/5. Worcs won by 5 wkts.
Hick 43 and 8–1–46–0; Dilley 11–0–65–2

18 June – RAL – Edgbaston – *v*. Warwickshire – Worcs 194/5, Warwicks 172/8. Worcs won by 22 runs.
Hick 35★ and 6–0–30–0, Dilley 8–0–30–3

21–3 June – BAC – Sheffield – *v*. Yorkshire – Yorks 249 and 280/4, Worcs 389/7. Match drawn.
Hick 150 and 10–3–22–1

22–7 June – Second Test – Lord's – England *v.* Australia –
England 286 and 359, Australia 528 and 119/4. Australia won
by six wkts.
Dilley 7 and 24, 34–3–141–2 and 10–2–27–1

24–6 June – BAC – New Road – *v.* Middlesex – Worcs 142 and
172, Middx 221 and 96/1. Middlesex won by nine wkts.
Hick 5 and 6

25 June – RAL – New Road – *v.* Middlesex – Worcs 143, Middx
144/5. Middx won by five wkts.
Hick 5 and 5–0–29–0

28 June – NW – March – *v.* Cambridgeshire – Cambs 202/4,
Worcs 206/1. Worcs won by nine wkts.
Hick 3–0–24–0 and 86*

1–4 July – BAC – Northampton – *v.* Northamptonshire –
Northants 256 and 158, Worcs 433. Worcs won by innings
and 19 runs.
Dilley 19–1–90–1 and 16–3–66–4, Hick 111, Dilley 1*

2 July – RAL – Tring – *v.* Northamptonshire – Northants 168,
Worcs 169/4. Worcs won by six wkts.
Hick 4

5–7 July – BAC – New Road – *v.* Warwickshire – Warwicks
265 and 47/0, Worcs 232. Match drawn.
Hick 4 and 4–0–16–0

6–11 July – Third Test – Edgbaston – England *v.* Australia –
Australia 424 and 158/2, England 242. Match drawn.
Dilley 31–3–123–2, 10–4–27–0 and 11*

8–11 July – BAC – Kidderminster – *v.* Leicestershire – Leics 180
and 80, Worcs 245 and 16/0. Worcs won by ten wkts.
Hick 41

9 July – RAL – New Road – *v.* Leicestershire – Leics 156/9, Worcs 157/4. Worcs won by six wkts.
Hick 13

12 July – NW – New Road – *v.* Derbyshire – Worcs 278/5, Derbys 240. Worcs won by 38 runs.
Hick 45, Dilley 10–4–28–1

16 July – RAL – Scarborough – *v.* Yorkshire – Yorks 204/7, Worcs 208/4. Worcs won by six wkts.
Dilley 8–0–45–0, Hick 18

19–21 July – BAC – Old Trafford – *v.* Lancashire – Worcs 191 and 199, Lancs 125 and 229. Worcs won by 36 runs.
Hick 21 and 16, Dilley 31 and 0*, 12.2–0–30–5 and 27.1–4–94–5

22–25 July – BAC – Hove – *v.* Sussex – Worcs 320 and 230/4, Sussex 301 and 250/6. Sussex won by four wkts.
Hick 0 and 110*, Dilley 6, Hick 14–4–35–3 and 11–0–83–2, Dilley 9–0–62–0 and 6–0–26–0

23 July – RAL – Hove – *v.* Sussex – Sussex 239/5, Worcs 225. Sussex won by 14 runs.
Hick 4–0–24–2 and 35

26–8 July – BAC – New Road – *v.* Surrey – Worcs 284 and 256/6 dec., Surrey 153 and 285. Worcs won by 103 runs.
Hick 9 and 85, 16–5–29–1

29 July–1 August – BAC – New Road – *v.* Kent – Worcs 402/6 dec. and 27/0, Kent 232 and 196. Worcs won by ten wkts.
Hick 147 and 6.4–2–7–1, 2–1–1–0

30 July – RAL – New Road – *v.* Kent – Kent 123, Worcs 126/3. Worcs won by seven wkts.
Hick 15

2 August – NW – New Road – *v*. Lancashire – Lancs 237/9, Worcs 241/3. Worcs won by seven wkts.
Dilley 12–3–47–0, Hick 90★

5–8 August – BAC – Colchester – *v*. Essex – Essex 208 and 323/9, Worcs 447/9 dec. Match drawn.
Hick 72, Dilley 9★, Hick 17–5–52–5 and 55–15–131–5, Dilley 7–2–14–1 and 16.2–3–47–0

6 August – RAL – Colchester – *v*. Essex – Essex 193, Worcs 197/4. Worcs won by six wkts.
Hick 54

9–11 August – BAC – Weston-super-Mare – *v*. Somerset – Somerset 240 and 145, Worcs 302/6 dec. and 87/1. Worcs won by nine wkts.
Dilley 25–5–101–3 and 14–2–44–0, Hick 27–11–40–3, 72 and 39★

12–15 August – BAC – Bournemouth – *v*. Hampshire – Worcs 325, Hants 137 and 97. Worcs won by innings and 91 runs.
Hick 44, Dilley 4★ and 11–3–32–3, 7–2–18–0, Hick 11–4–19–1 and 7–4–6–1

13 August – RAL – Bournemouth – *v*. Hampshire – Worcs 149, Hants 147/9. Worcs won by two runs.
Hick 30 and 8–0–24–1

16 August – NW – Edgbaston – *v*. Warwickshire – Warwicks 220/9, Worcs 120. Warwicks won by 100 runs.
Hick 12–0–43–0 and 7

20 August – RAL – New Road – *v*. Somerset – Worcs 205/5, Somerset 190/7. Worcs won by 12 runs.
Hick 81 and 6–0–46–1

24–7 August – BAC – New Road – *v*. Somerset – Somerset 338 and 161/6 dec., Worcs 200/5 dec. and 302/5. Worcs won by five wkts.
Hick 13–5–21–1, 86 and 136★

29–31 August – BAC – New Road – *v*. Gloucestershire – Worcs 248 and 213, Gloucs 206 and 124. Worcs won by 131 runs to retain county championship.
Hick 19 and 20, Dilley 6★ and 1, 13–2–51–3 and 8.4–2–22–4

4 September – WF – Scarborough – *v*. Essex – Worcs 221/4, Essex 225/2. Essex won by eight wkts.
Hick 7 and 9–0–42–0

6 September – RAC – New Road – *v*. Essex – Essex 211/7, Worcs 110. Essex won by 101 runs.
Hick 0

13–16 September – BAC – Pontypridd – *v*. Glamorgan – Glamorgan 230/9. Match abandoned as a draw.
Dilley 10–1–40–0, Hick 8–2–12–1

BRITANNIC ASSURANCE CHAMPIONSHIP
FINAL TABLE
Win=16 pts

	P	W	L	D	Bt	Bl	Pts
WORCESTERSHIRE (1)	22	12	3	7	44	83	319
Essex (3)	22	13	2	7	59	71	313★
Middlesex (8)	22	9	2	11	50	72	266
Lancashire (9)	22	8	5	9	57	65	250
Northamptonshire (12)	22	7	8	7	47	63	222
Hampshire (15)	22	6	8	8	55	65	216
Derbyshire (14)	22	6	6	10	45	75	216
Warwickshire (6)	22	5	4	13	44	75	207†
Gloucestershire (10)	22	6	11	5	38	70	204
Sussex (16)	22	4	4	14	60	68	192
Nottinghamshire (5)	22	4	6	10	54	65	190★
Surrey (4)	22	4	7	11	50	69	183
Leicestershire (7)	22	4	8	10	43	74	181
Somerset (11)	22	4	6	12	50	54	168
Kent (2)	22	3	8	11	53	53	154
Yorkshire (13)	22	3	9	10	41	60	149
Glamorgan (17)	22	3	6	13	38	59	145

★ *25 pts deducted for substandard pitch.*
† *includes 8 pts for drawn match in which scores finished level.*
1988 positions in brackets.

REFUGE ASSURANCE LEAGUE – FINAL TABLE

Win=4 pts. Tie/No result=2 pts.

	P	W	L	T	NR	Pts
LANCASHIRE (3)	16	12	2	0	2	52
Worcestershire (1)	16	11	4	0	1	46
Essex (10)	16	11	4	0	1	46
Nottinghamshire (17)	16	9	6	0	1	38
Derbyshire (12)	16	9	6	0	1	38
Surrey (5)	16	9	7	0	0	36
Northamptonshire (14)	16	8	6	0	2	36
Hampshire (9)	16	8	6	1	1	36
Middlesex (4)	16	8	7	1	0	34
Somerset (12)	16	7	8	1	0	30
Yorkshire (8)	16	7	9	0	0	28
Kent (7)	16	7	9	0	0	28
Sussex (14)	16	6	8	1	1	28
Warwickshire (10)	16	5	10	0	1	22
Leicestershire (14)	16	5	10	0	1	22
Gloucestershire (2)	16	3	13	0	0	12
Glamorgan (5)	16	2	12	0	2	12

First four counties qualified for Refuge Assurance Cup semi-finals.

Where points equal, positions decided on (a) most wins, (b) most away wins, (c) run rate.

Worcs had 6 away wins to Essex's 4, while Notts' run rate (4.691 per over) was superior to Derbyshire's (4.238), both sides having 4 away wins.

1988 positions in brackets.

WORCESTERSHIRE CHAMPIONSHIP AVERAGES

BATTING	M	I	NO	Runs	HS	Av	100	50
G. A. Hick	22	35	5	1595	150	53.17	5	8
T. S. Curtis	16	27	2	1213	156	48.52	4	7
P. A. Neale	21	31	7	911	98	37.96	0	7
S. J. Rhodes	20	29	13	589	83	36.81	0	2
C. M. Tolley	5	6	2	120	37	30.00	0	0
M. J. Weston	14	22	3	473	74	24.89	0	2
P. Bent	13	22	0	530	144	24.09	1	2
S. M. McEwan	11	9	3	139	28★	23.17	0	0
G. R. Dilley	12	14	10	88	31	22.00	0	0
D. B. D'Oliveira	22	34	1	723	63	21.91	0	5
S. R. Lampitt	9	7	2	99	46	19.80	0	0
N. V. Radford	16	20	1	319	66★	16.79	0	1
I. T. Botham	12	18	1	276	73	16.24	0	1
G. J. Lord	8	13	2	170	54	15.45	0	1
R. K. Illingworth	22	24	1	321	71	13.96	0	2
D. A. Leatherdale	7	8	1	93	25	13.29	0	0
P. J. Newport	6	8	1	86	27	12.29	0	0
S. R. Bevins	2	2	1	11	6★	11.00	0	0
A. P. Pridgeon	4	4	1	24	19★	8.00	0	0

BOWLING	O	M	R	W	Av	BB	5i	10m
S. R. Lampitt	219.5	56	526	31	16.97	5–32	2	0
S. M. McEwan	368.3	82	999	52	19.21	6–34	3	0
G. R. Dilley	321.2	58	1062	55	19.31	5–28	5	1
P. J. Newport	181	28	525	27	19.44	5–73	1	0
G. A. Hick	214.4	65	519	26	19.96	5–52	2	1
R. K. Illingworth	429.4	176	857	40	21.43	5–23	1	0
I. T. Botham	386.4	86	1122	51	22.00	7–85	3	1
N. V. Radford	516.2	105	1575	67	23.51	6–59	3	0
M. J. Weston	141.3	44	365	12	30.42	3–21	0	0

Also bowled: T. S. Curtis 4.3–0–10–0; P. A. Neale 1–0–8–0;
A. P. Pridgeon 47.5–14–95–3; C. M. Tolley 61–16–138–1.

HUNDREDS (10)

5 – G. A. Hick: 150 *v*. Yorks (Sheffield); 111 *v*. Northants (Northampton); 110★ *v*. Sussex (Hove); 147 *v*. Kent (Worcester);
   136★ *v*. Somerset (Worcester).
4 – T. S. Curtis: 102 *v*. Glos (Bristol); 140★ *v*. Glamorgan
   (Worcester); 102 *v*. Sussex (Hove); 156 *v*. Essex (Colchester).
1 – P. Bent: 144 *v*. Kent (Worcester).

PICTURE
ACKNOWLEDGEMENTS

The authors and publishers would like to thank the following:
Roger Hooper: page 7 *below*
Les Jacques: page 5 *above left* and *right*, page 6 *below*, page 7 *above
right* and *left*
Mark Leech: page 8 *above*
Graham Morris: page 1, 2, 3, 4, 5 *below left* and *right*
Adrian Murrell, All-Sport: page 6 *above*
Press Association: page 8 *below*